Get
Ready
to Learn

Nancy Champion Chupp

THOMAS NELSON PUBLISHERS
Nashville • Atlanta • London • Vancouver

*To my mom, Christine Champion Chupp,
and my dad, James Merrill Chupp, Sr.
You were wonderful teachers.*

Acknowledgments

*Special thanks to Marsha Madden Jones,
M.A., Ed., and Frank A. Green, M.A., Eng.,
for their editorial assistance.*

Published in Nashville, Tennessee, by Thomas Nelson, Inc., Publishers, and distributed in Canada by Word Communications, Ltd., Richmond, British Columbia.

Library of Congress Cataloging-in-Publication Data

Chupp, Nancy Champion, 1945–
    Get ready to learn / Nancy Champion Chupp.
        p.   cm.
    ISBN 0-8407-9225-5 (pbk.)
    1. Readiness for school.   2. Education, Preschool—Parent participation.   3. Education, Preschool—Activity programs.
I. Title.
LB1132.C49   1994
649'.68—dc20

94–16042
CIP

Printed in the United States of America.

1 2 3 4 5 6 — 99 98 97 96 95 94

Introduction

The activities in *Get Ready to Learn* are designed to introduce specific skills to your child. The book suggests using typical household items in activities that are already part of your daily routine. The primary focus is on you, **THE PARENT.** Care is given to explain to you **HOW TO TEACH YOUR CHILD** each concept that is introduced. The secondary focus is on your **PRESCHOOL CHILD.** Emphasis is given to the mental and physical preparation that he/she will need upon entering kindergarten.

Integrating Fun Daily Activities into Your Family's Lifestyle

Your child will learn and develop best through **MENTAL** and **PHYSICAL EXPERIENCES** and **REPETITION.** Children need to be shown and introduced to many concepts. After that, repetition seems to be the learning key! Each concept in this book is presented many times to ensure that your child internalizes and masters it.

Mental and Physical Activity

Encouraging Your Child's Natural Desire to Learn

As a teacher, I was frequently asked, "What can I do at home to help my child learn?" Since a child's education starts **BEFORE** kindergarten, I perceived a need for a book like *Get Ready to Learn*. The book obviously had to focus on the skills needed by the preschooler. *But more importantly, it had to focus on the needs of the parent. If the book did not fit into daily routines and lifestyles, the parent was not going to use it!* After recognizing those conditions, I focused the book on two criteria:

1. Giving you a step-by-step mechanism to dramatically influence your child's educational start.
2. Giving your child a particular skill base before entering kindergarten.

Get Ready to Learn is designed to develop skills your child will need in order to be READY for kindergarten. It focuses on the readiness skills presented in the *Santa Clara Inventory of Developmental Tasks,* published by Zaner-Bloser. Having developed these skills and learned certain basic concepts, your child will enter kindergarten on better footing and with more confidence. I trust that *Get Ready to Learn* will instill in your child an "I can do it" attitude toward learning!

Developing Mental and Physical Abilities in Your Child

READ TO YOUR CHILD DAILY

It is the **MOST IMPORTANT** way in which you can help your child learn to read! By reading to your child, you are instilling in him/her a **LOVE FOR BOOKS.** Set aside one day a week to visit the library!

GIVE DAILY CHOICES

Give your child a choice *when you can.* Offer your child two good alternatives. Your child wins with either selection! This activity helps develop his/her decision-making skills. Success in decision making will help increase your child's self-confidence.

LISTEN TO YOUR CHILD

Once a day, try to sit with your child one-on-one *(maybe at bedtime)* and listen to his/her concerns, successes, and/or failures. Let your child know that he/she can tell you **ANYTHING!** However, prepare yourself!

ASK YOUR CHILD QUESTIONS

Let your child know that you are interested in what he/she is doing. Dinnertime is a good time for asking questions—What? Where? When? Who? and How?

PRAISE ENCOURAGES ALL OF US

Your child desires **YOUR** praise most of all! Remember to give your child positive responses such as "Yes!" or "That's a good try!" Make encouraging statements to your child, **ESPECIALLY** when he/she is trying something new!

CHILDREN NEED HUGS

You can give hugs for many good reasons, but most of all, give lots of them! Hugging many times a day helps instill in your child the feeling of **value.** It is very important that your child feel worth in order to develop positive self-esteem.

Mental Activity

Tell your child, "Today is **Sunday.** It is the **first** day of the week; a week is made up of **7 days.**"

The color of the week is **RED.**

Have your child look at the red color example on the book cover. Then have him/her point out 3 items in the kitchen that are red.

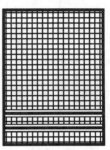

When your child makes a correct choice, **praise** by saying, *"Yes, that is a red apple!"* Or when your child picks up an orange *(instead of red)* book, **correct** your child *(without criticism)* in this way: *"That book is orange."*   *"Look at the red example again."*   *"Can you find something in the kitchen that is red?"*

Don't point out that your child is wrong; instead correct your child, and then ask the same question again! *The goal is to encourage your child to **take a chance** with the activity. If he/she always has to be **right,** he/she will soon stop trying.*

After your child has found 3 red items, ask him/her to tell you the **name** of each of these items.

Then ask your child to **describe** each item using complete sentences: *"I will eat the red apple."*   *"We dry our dishes with the red dish towel."*   *"Mom reads the red cookbook."*

Physical Activity

While outside, have your child hop in place and count while he/she hops.

How many hops did your child make hopping on both feet?

Have your child **hop** on his/her **right** foot. **Count** together. How many hops were made?

Have your child **hop** on his/her **left** foot. **Count** together. How many hops were made?

Ask your child if he/she hopped **more** on his/her left or right foot.

Ask your child if he/she hopped **less** on his/her left or right foot.

black   red

Tape the word *left* (in black) on your child's left shoe.

Tape the word *right* (in red) on your child's right shoe.

Parent—Did You Remember To

| HUG | READ TOGETHER | GIVE CHOICES | LISTEN | ASK QUESTIONS | PRAISE | HUG |

1

COUNTING BOX

Mental Activity

"Today is **Monday,** the **second** day of the week; a week has **7 days.**" *(Always repeat this idea to your child.)*

Start a COUNTING BOX.

That is a box full of small items that your child can use for counting, color recognition, and memory activities. For example, thread spools, crayons, bottle tops, and milk bottle caps can be used. **Use whatever you feel is safe for your child to handle.**

Have your child TOUCH and COUNT 3 items from the COUNTING BOX.

Put 3 items on the left side of a table. Make a line in the center of the table *(perhaps with a ribbon or a piece of yarn)*. Have your child **TOUCH and COUNT** the 3 items. That means to have your child pick up an item from the left side of the ribbon and say, "ONE." Then have your child put item #1 down on the right side of the ribbon.

Have your child pick up item #2 and count, "TWO." Then have your child put item #2 down on the right side of the ribbon.

Have your child pick up the third item and count, "THREE."

Show your child what you mean until he/she understands TOUCH and COUNT. Give your child 4 items. Can he/she **TOUCH and COUNT** to 4? How high can your child count? If your child gets stumped on 5, you know that counting to 5 has to be mastered before your child can count to 6. The goal for your child is to be able to count to 20.

one

two

three

Physical Activity

Have your child practice pouring water from one plastic bottle into another plastic bottle during bath time.

You can make this activity more and more challenging by using various size bottles *(cleaned-up shampoo bottles, etc.)*.

Pouring back and forth helps your child develop muscle control of his/her hand.

Pouring also helps your child develop eye-hand coordination.

Parent—Did You Remember To

HUG

READ TOGETHER

GIVE CHOICES

LISTEN

ASK QUESTIONS

PRAISE

HUG

Mental Activity _____

"Today is **Tuesday,** the **third** day of the week; a week has **7 days.**"
(Always repeat this idea to your child.)

Practice handwriting with your child. Show your child how to hold a crayon or pencil.

Always hand your child the pencil in the middle of his/her body. He/she will reach for the pencil with his/her dominant hand.

When your child first begins trying to draw or write, he/she will have much less trouble if the following GRIP is used.

1. The back of the pencil rests on the curve of your child's hand.
2. Your child grasps the pencil with his/her thumb and second finger.
3. Your child's index finger (first finger) rests on top of the pencil.

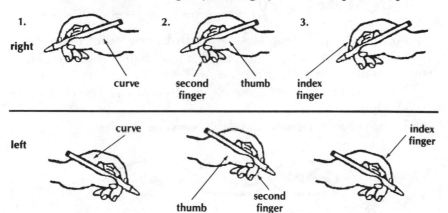

Show your child how to position paper for writing.

left hand

right hand

The left-handed child needs to be taught to keep his/her paper *(angled right)* and his/her hand in the proper position.
The hand and pencil point should rest *below* the writing line.

The right-handed child needs to be taught to keep his/her paper in the proper position *(angled left).*

Physical Activity _____

Have your child bounce a ball 1 time, 2 times, 3 times, 4 times, and 5 times.

Day 4

WEEK

1

Mental Activity

Tell your child, "Today is **Wednesday,** the **fourth** day of the week; a week has **7 days.**"

After the evening bath, have your child choose what to wear tomorrow. Mornings are usually very busy, so this activity can solve one of tomorrow morning's problems! Since your child might make inappropriate choices *(swimsuit in winter),* say to your child, *"Would you like to wear this blue shirt and pants, or this red shirt and shorts?"*

In that way you are guiding your child's choices, but you are giving him/her the chance to gain confidence in his/her ability to make a decision!

Physical Activity

Have your child walk heel-to-toe from one point to another.

Count out loud while your child is walking heel-to-toe. How many steps did your child take?

Walking this way requires balance. You may need to show your child how to use his/her arms for balance.

This activity helps promote your child's overall coordination.

Don't forget the pouring activity. Keep adding different size plastic containers.

Parent—Did You Remember To

  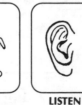 

HUG   READ TOGETHER   GIVE CHOICES   LISTEN   ASK QUESTIONS   PRAISE   HUG

4

Mental Activity _____

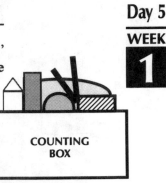

"Today is **Thursday,** the **fifth** day of the week; a week has **7 days.**"

From the **COUNTING BOX, select 3 items. Put them on the kitchen table.**

Ask your child to find 3 items from the box that are JUST LIKE the ones on the table. You want the items EXACTLY the same.

If you put a red milk cap on the table, and your child selects a *blue* milk cap from the box, ask your child if the 2 milk caps look exactly alike.

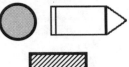

If he/she says, *"Yes,"* ask him/her if the colors are the same. If necessary, tell your child the names of the cap colors, and ask him/her to find a *red* milk cap.

Remember, you are not trying for instant RIGHT answers.

When your child is not sure, guide him/her to discover the answer for himself/herself.

You want your child to TAKE A CHANCE *(with these mental activities).* Children will TRY or take MENTAL RISKS when they feel that it is SAFE to do so.

Set up a new pattern of 3.

Let your child look at the new pattern for 5 to 10 seconds.

Put the items back in the box.

Then ask your child to **find the same 3 items** from the box.

Physical Activity _____

Today, have your child practice jumping over a stick or a rope.

First **Facing** the stick, your child should jump over the stick and back, using **both** feet.

Second Have your child stand with his/her **right side** toward the stick.

Have your child jump over the stick and back on his/her **right** foot only.

Third Have your child stand with his/her **left side** toward the stick.

Have your child jump over the stick and back on his/her **left** foot only.

Mental Activity

Tell your child, "Today is **Friday.** It's the **sixth** day of the week; a week has **7 days.**"

RED is the color of the week.

Since it is Friday, perhaps there is a trip to the grocery store or Laundromat. On the way to the store, have your child look for red vehicles. Remember to **praise,** *"Yes, that was a red truck!"*

Or you may need to correct and ask again, *"That car was orange. Can you find a red car?"*

Physical Activity

While at the grocery store, see if the store has 2 empty cardboard boxes that you could take home.

Use the boxes for CATEGORY BOXES.

Help your child separate recyclable cans and plastics into the category of cans and the category of plastics.

TOUCH and COUNT the category of cans.

TOUCH and COUNT the category of plastics.

Which category has **more?** Which category has **less?**

Have your child **touch** a can and a plastic bottle. Ask your child, "Do these items feel the **same** or **different?**"

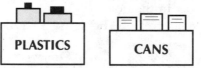

Show your child how to draw a line, a cross, a square, and a circle.

Show your child how to draw a **line.** Use a starting point; then pull a fat crayon to the right.

Let your child draw a line. Give him/her a starting point, and remind him/her to start at the left and pull right.

Show your child how to draw a **cross** *(follow the diagram).* Let your child make a cross. Remind him/her to start at the left and pull right, start at the top and pull down.

Show your child how to draw a **square** *(follow the diagram).* Let your child make a square. Remind him/her to start at the left and pull right, start at the top and pull down.

Show your child how to draw a **circle** *(follow the diagram).* Let your child make a circle. Give him/her a starting point. Remind him/her to start at the top and pull down, moving from left to right.

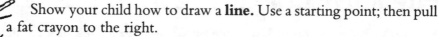

Mental Activity _____

"It is **Saturday.** It is the **seventh** day of **RED** week; a week has **7 days.**" Find red while in the park, the yard, or the library.

Write the name of each day of the week on a 3″ x 5″ note card.

Have your child TOUCH and COUNT the "days of the week" note cards.

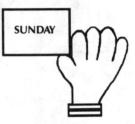

Your child picks up the first card, says, "One," puts #1 down.

Your child picks up the second card, says, "Two," puts #2 down, and so on.

Go through the cards again. This time read the sequence of the days of the week.

Tell your child, *"This is the card for Sunday; this is the card for Monday; this is the card for Tuesday,"* and so on. Then practice together saying the days of the week **in order** *(Sunday, Monday, Tuesday, etc.).*

Read the "days of the week" cards to your child every day, in sequence. Ask your child to repeat the sequence with you.

Physical Activity _____

Place 2 empty cardboard boxes outside. Set up each box with a CATEGORY.

Put a pinecone in box 1—*this box's category will be pinecones.*
Put a pebble in box 2—*this box's category will be pebbles.*

Ask your child to find those 2 items in the yard, then put those items into the correct CATEGORY BOX. *Use any 2 items found in your yard (or the park) that you feel would be safe for your child to handle.*

Have your child TOUCH and COUNT each of the 2 categories.

1, 2, 3, 4, 5, 6,

Which category had **more?** Which category had **less?**

Have your child describe each item.
The pinecones are brown and have sharp points.
The pebbles are smooth and are heavy.

Mental Activity _____

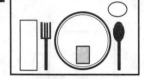

"Today is **Sunday,** the **first** day of the week; a week has **7 days.**"

Parent, while you are making a meal, put plates on the table for your family.

Ask your child to **match** one spoon to the **right** side of each plate all the way around the table. Then have your child **match** any or all of the following items to each plate:

One fork to the **left** of each plate

One plastic cup/glass to the **top** of each spoon

One bread slice on the **bottom** of each plate

(Remember, place one item at a time all the way around the table.)

The color for the week is YELLOW. Show your child **yellow** from the color chart on the book cover. Ask your child to find something in the COUNTING BOX that is yellow.

Physical Activity _____

Have your child continue to practice drawing/writing a line, a cross, a square, and a circle.

Have your child follow these 3 directions:

Run to the fence. Turn around 1 time. Crawl to the tree.

Read together each day. Point to each word as you read.

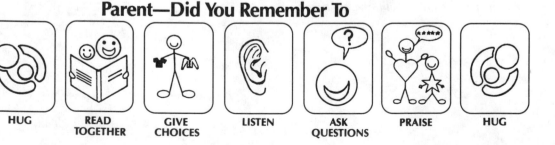

Parent—Did You Remember To

| HUG | READ TOGETHER | GIVE CHOICES | LISTEN | ASK QUESTIONS | PRAISE | HUG |

8

Mental Activity ────────────────

"Today is **Monday,** the **second** day of the week; a week has **7 days.**"
Use the COUNTING BOX COLLECTION for a memory game.

Put 3 items on the table: *maybe a yellow juice lid, a red milk cap, and a blue crayon.* Let your child look at the articles for 4 or 5 seconds. Put the items back into the counting box.

Ask your child to find the same 3 items from the box and put them on the table.

If your child cannot remember, try the game with 2 items.

After the child finds the items, have your child identify each color, **describe** each item's use, and **TOUCH and COUNT** the items.

Set up another group of 2 or 3 for more memory practice.
Keep adding to your collection of items for the counting box.
They must be items that you feel are safe for your child to handle: large buttons that could not be swallowed, large juice caps, spools of thread, crayons, container lids, barrettes, and so on.

This week's color is yellow. Find 3 yellow items in the kitchen. Then TOUCH and COUNT.
*Remember to **praise:** "Yes, you found a yellow cup, a yellow flower, and a yellow pot holder!"*
*Remember to **correct** and **ask again** if necessary:*
"That is a green cup. Can you find something in the room that is yellow?"

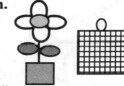

Physical Activity ────────────────

Parent, draw a straight line on a piece of paper. Then have your child use a pair of children's scissors to cut on the line.
It may be helpful to show your child the hand motion used in cutting.
Show your child how to put his/her thumb and first finger together, then apart, together, then apart.
Supervise your child at all times while he/she is using scissors.

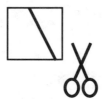

Today, see if your child can balance on each foot for 5 seconds *(then maybe 10 seconds!).*
But **first,** with masking tape and a **red** marker put the word *right* on your child's right shoe, and with masking tape and a **black** marker put the word *left* on your child's left shoe.
Count out loud while your child is balancing on his/her **left** foot and then on his/her **right** foot. On which foot could your child stand **longer?**

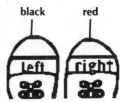

Mental Activity _____

left
left margin
Day 3

WEEK

2

"Today is **Tuesday,** the **third** day of the week; a week has **7 days.**"

Give your child a choice for breakfast: "Would you like toast or cereal for breakfast?"

You want to avoid a "no" answer from your preschooler.

With a choice question, "Would you like toast or cereal?" *you are avoiding confrontation, and you are teaching your child to consider choices and make a decision!*

Children need to learn how to make choices. Through this practice, your child will gain confidence in his/her **ability to make a decision. Give choices** whenever possible. You direct the choices so that **either selection** will be **appropriate and successful** for your child.

The color for the week is yellow.

Have your child **find 3 yellow items** from a jewelry box, scarf drawer, or linen closet. *(Make sure that there **are** 3 yellow items.)*

Have your child **TOUCH and COUNT** the yellow items.

Have your child **describe** the items: *"The pin has three yellow balloons,"* or *"The scarf has two big yellow stars."*

Physical Activity _____

With the word *right* **taped on your child's right shoe, have your child walk up 3 steps, right foot first.** *As your child is going up the steps, say,* **"Right,"** *with each* **right** *step taken.*

Then with the word *left* **on your child's left shoe, have your child walk up 3 steps, left foot first.** *As your child is going up the steps, say,* **"Left,"** *with each* **left** *step taken.*

Parent—Did You Remember To

| HUG | READ TOGETHER | GIVE CHOICES | LISTEN | ASK QUESTIONS | PRAISE | HUG |

Mental Activity

"Today is **Wednesday,** the **fourth** day of the week; a week has **7 days.**"

Today, label items found in the kitchen.

Using Magic Markers and 3″ x 5″ cards *or paper squares,* **write the names** of kitchen items about 2″ high. **Tape** the name tag on each item. **Touch** each label and **tell** your child the name written on each label. For example, *"This is the word for refrigerator."*

Label the stove, the chairs, and the microwave—as many things as you can. Leave the labels on the items.

Daily, point to each word and read the word to your child. He/she will soon realize that these symbols or **words** stand for actual things.

table

stove

chair

microwave

refrigerator

Physical Activity

Marching is today's physical activity.

Tape the words *left* and *right* on the tops of your child's shoes.

Remind your child of the code: left is black; right is red.

Show your child how to march. Then march together from one point to another.

While marching, you will be calling out, **"Left, right, left, right."**

You will need to watch your child carefully to see that he/she is using the correct foot.

black   red

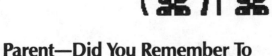

Parent—Did You Remember To

 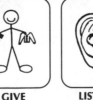   

HUG   **READ TOGETHER**   **GIVE CHOICES**   **LISTEN**   **ASK QUESTIONS**   **PRAISE**   **HUG**

Mental Activity

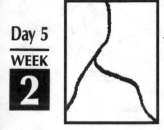

Day 5

WEEK

2

"Today is **Thursday,** the **fifth** day of the week; a week has **7 days.**"
Today, parent, make a puzzle for your child from a used cereal box.

Save an empty cereal box and cut out the front picture. Show your child the picture, then cut the picture into 3 pieces. Let your child put the puzzle together. Save the pieces in a bag, and start a box puzzle collection for your child.

The child may need to see the picture each time before putting the puzzle together, so put the puzzle together for your child first, mix up the pieces, and then let your child put the puzzle together.

Physical Activity

Every day, have your child write/draw a line, a cross, a square, and a circle.

Watch your child.

Is he/she holding the crayon/pencil correctly?

Is he/she starting at the left and pulling the crayon/pencil to the right?

Is he/she starting at the top and pulling down?

Have your child write/draw these items several times.

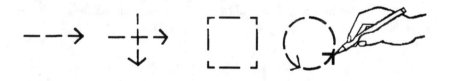

Have your child roll and kick a ball. Have your child try to kick with his/her **right** foot. Have your child try to kick with his/her **left** foot.

Parent—Did You Remember To

HUG   READ TOGETHER   GIVE CHOICES   LISTEN   ASK QUESTIONS   PRAISE   HUG

Mental Activity

"Today is **Friday,** the **sixth** day of the week; a week has **7 days.**"
Read the name of each labeled item in the kitchen.

Ask your child to **describe** each item after you read its label. Give him/her examples: *"The refrigerator is big and white. It is cold inside the refrigerator. We store food in the refrigerator."*

If he/she gets stumped, ask questions that will help him/her describe the item:

"What does it look like? What color is it?"
"Does it make a sound? What does it sound like?"
"What does it smell like?"
"How does it feel?"
"How do we use this item?"

These exercises in vocabulary will increase your child's awareness of the items around him/her.

All these experiences are very important to your child's later success in reading.

| sink |
| door |
| table |
| cabinet |
| faucet |
| lamp |
| stove |
| chair |

Day 6
WEEK
2

Physical Activity

Mark your child's right hand with a red *R* using nontoxic Magic Marker *(or write on tape and put it on your child's hand).*

Today's physical activity will be **tapping.**

Using your **right** hand, tap out a 4-beat pattern on the table *(1 hard hit; 2 soft hits; 1 hard hit).*

See if your child can **repeat the same pattern.**

Make up other patterns using your **right** hand. *Keep reminding your child that he/she is using his/her right hand.*

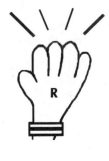

Make a beanbag with dried beans and a washcloth.

 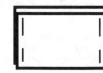

| **fold the washcloth in half** | **sew up the sides** | **pour in the beans** | **sew up the top** |

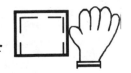

Using the new beanbag, have some fun outside with your child playing catch.

Mental Activity _____

"Today is **Saturday,** the **seventh** day of the week; a week has **7 days.**"

Today, your child will use his/her ears instead of his/her eyes to identify things.

Have your child close his/her eyes and then identify running water, a door opening, paper tearing, a bell ringing, and a clock ticking.

Play the same game outside. Can your child identify bouncing balls, breaking twigs, and raking leaves?

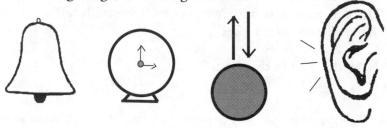

This week's color is YELLOW. Can your child find something yellow outside? It can be anything: flowers, fall leaves, a flowerpot, a chair, a neighbor's house.

Physical Activity _____

Have your child walk a 5-foot straight line *(maybe a crack in the sidewalk)* **heel-to-toe.**

Your child will have to balance himself/herself while trying to walk on the line.

Show your child how to use his/her arms to help maintain his/her balance.

Have your child count his/her steps. He/she will probably need your help while counting.

Parent—Did You Remember To

HUG

READ
TOGETHER

GIVE
CHOICES

LISTEN

ASK
QUESTIONS

PRAISE

HUG

Mental Activity _____

"Today is **Sunday,** the **first** day of the week; a week has **7 days.**"

The color for the week is BLUE. **Have your child find 3 blue items from his/her closet or drawer.**

Have your child **describe** each item to you: *"This shirt is blue." "These socks have blue stripes." "The pj's have blue bears."*
Use a Styrofoam egg carton for counting and sorting.

Cut off 2 cups of a regular 12–cup egg carton. With a marker, write the numbers 1 through 10 on the egg carton cups. Use dried lima beans *(or any rather large dried bean)* for counting pieces.

Then have your child **TOUCH and COUNT** to 5. Have your child **pick up** 1 lima bean. **Put** that bean into space "1," then **say,** "ONE."

Continue the same way with the second lima bean. **Pick up** the bean, **put** that bean into space "2," and **say,** "TWO."

Repeat this activity through the number 5.

If your child has **no** trouble with the activity, continue adding one more number until your child gets to 10.

(This is a great activity for your child's hand-muscle control and eye-hand coordination.)

Physical Activity _____

Have your child write/draw a line, a cross, a square, and a circle. *(Your child should start from the left and pull right, or from the top and pull down.)*

Have your child draw a picture of himself/herself. Put a date on the picture and keep it.

Have your child explain the picture to you.

(Write your child's description on the picture: what he/she is wearing and what he/she is doing.)

15

Mental Activity _____

Day 2

WEEK

3

"Today is **Monday,** the **second** day of the week; a week has **7 days.**"

The color for the week is BLUE. Find 3 blue items from pictures in a magazine, catalogue, or book.

Have your child **describe** the 3 blue items that were found: *"The van has a blue stripe."* *"The house has a blue roof."* *"The sky is blue."*

Today, with a shoelace and pasta *(rigatoni or ziti)* **make a bracelet.**

Have your child **STRING and COUNT** 8 pieces of pasta. Then tie the bracelet on your child's **right** wrist. Tell your child that you are tying the bracelet on his/her **wrist** *(did he/she know that word?).*

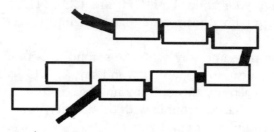

Play a FOLLOWING DIRECTIONS game. Ask your child to

raise his/her **right** arm into the air.
put his/her **right** arm behind his/her back.
put his/her **right** arm at his/her right side.
put your **left** arm behind your back.

*Did your child remember **left and right?** (Remind your child that he/she has a bracelet on his/her **right wrist.**)*

Physical Activity _____

After bath time, have your child pick out clothes for the next morning. *(This practice will help make mornings less confusing.)*

You may need to give him/her a choice between 2 outfits. *(Would you like to wear this or this?)*

If your child can make **appropriate choices,** let him/her select the outfit by himself/herself.

You may need to **tell your child:** *"Tomorrow is a school day; you need school clothes."*

It's **blue** week. Ask your child to pick out something **blue** to wear tomorrow.

Mental Activity

"Today is **Tuesday,** the **third** day of the week; a week has **7 days.**"
Today, your child will sort 3 objects.

1. Use 3 small boxes.
2. Find 3 kinds of objects to sort (perhaps you could use buttons, pennies, and milk bottle caps).
3. Put the collection of sorting items in a pile **on** the table.
4. As a guide for your child, put an extra button, penny, and bottle cap into each box.
5. Tell your child to **sort the group of items into** *categories.*

Ask your child to TOUCH and COUNT each *category.*
Which *category* had the **most?** Which *category* had the **least?**
Put a button, a penny, and a milk cap on the table. Ask your child, *"Which is **biggest?**"   "Which is **smallest?**"   "Of these three items, which one is in the **middle?**"*

pennies

buttons

milk bottle caps

Day 3
WEEK
3

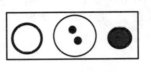

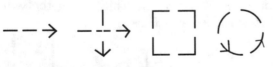

Physical Activity

Ask your child to touch his/her toe, elbow, arm, wrist, stomach, head, eye, ear, nose, and mouth.
Play this game with your child so that he/she will know the names of the various parts of his/her body.

Your child will continue to practice writing a line, a cross, a square, and a circle.

$$-- \rightarrow \quad -\!\!\!\!\mid \rightarrow \quad \square \quad \bigcirc$$

Parent—Did You Remember To

HUG   READ TOGETHER   GIVE CHOICES   LISTEN   ASK QUESTIONS   PRAISE   HUG

Mental Activity _____

"Today is **Wednesday,** the **fourth** day of the week; a week has **7 days.**"

Today, have your child practice NESTING bowls, pans, or measuring cups (*any items that you have that fit inside each other—like 3 sizes of bowls*).

1. Put the 3 nesting bowls on the table.
2. Show your child how to nest the bowls.
3. Then ask your child to nest the bowls.
4. NOW ask your child,
   "Which bowl is **biggest?**"
   "Which bowl is **smallest?**"
   "Which bowl is in the **middle?**"
   "What **color** are the bowls?"
   "Which bowl is on **top?**"
   "Which bowl is on the **bottom?**"
   "Which bowl is in the **middle?**"

smallest
middle
biggest

top
middle
bottom

Physical Activity _____

Today's physical activity will be to have your child follow directions.

1. Ask your child to climb **over** a chair and to walk **through** the kitchen door and **down** the steps.
2. Ask your child to walk **up** the steps, **through** the door, and **around** the table and to crawl **under** a chair.
3. Make up directions for your child using the words *over, under, around, through, up,* and *down.*

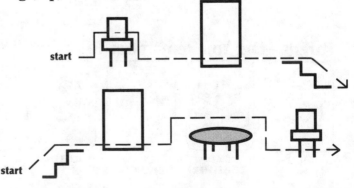

start

start

Mental Activity

"Today is **Thursday,** the **fifth** day of the week; a week has **7 days.**"
Label these things in your child's room: mirror, bed, lamp, dresser, and drawer.

1. Tape the written label **on** each item.
2. Point to each label and read the word to your child. *(You want your child to understand that letter symbols are put together to make words and that words stand for actual items.)*
3. See if your child can point to the various labels and tell you what the words stand for.

| MIRROR |
| BED |
| LAMP |
| DRESSER |
| DRAWER |

Day 5
WEEK
3

This week's color is BLUE. Have your child do the following:

1. **Find** 3 blue items in the bedroom.
2. **TOUCH and COUNT** the blue items.
3. **Describe** each blue item to you: *"This is a blue pencil eraser." "The crayon is blue." "My scarf has blue lines."*

Physical Activity

Make a box puzzle with your child (cake mix, brownie box).

1. Cut the box front into 5 pieces. Put the pieces together for your child.
2. Mix up the pieces, and have your child put the puzzle together.
3. Save the pieces in a bag for your child's box puzzle collection.

Have your child practice writing/drawing a line, a cross, a square, and a circle.

Parent—Did You Remember To

HUG

READ TOGETHER

GIVE CHOICES

LISTEN

ASK QUESTIONS

PRAISE

HUG

Mental Activity _____

"Today is **Friday,** the **sixth** day of the week; a week has **7 days.**"
This week's color is BLUE; let your child identify the color blue while at the grocery store.

Does your child remember the color **red** and the color **yellow?**

When you come home from the grocery store, have your child identify two categories:

1. **Canned goods**
   Have your child **sort** through the groceries to find canned items.
   Your child is selecting **1 type of item**—the category of **cans.**
   Have your child **TOUCH and COUNT** the number of cans found.

2. **Bathroom items**
   Have your child **sort** through the groceries to find bathroom items *(soap, shampoo, tissue, toothpaste).* This time your child will have lots of **different items** that will fit into the **category** of **bathroom items.** Have your child **TOUCH and COUNT** the number of bathroom items found.

Physical Activity _____

Have your child help you with yard or park cleanup by giving him/her 3 directions to follow:

1. **Pick up** paper trash and put it in a bag.
2. **Rake** leaves and put them in a box.
3. **Water** 3 small plants.

paper trash   leaves

Parent—Did You Remember To

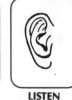

HUG   READ TOGETHER   GIVE CHOICES   LISTEN   ASK QUESTIONS   PRAISE   HUG

Mental Activity _____

"Today is **Saturday,** the **seventh** day of the week; a week has **7 days.**"

While on your way to the park, the library, or the store, ask your child to point out/identify these buildings:

Gas station
Grocery store
Church
School
Department store

Have your child draw THE FAMILY.
Date the picture.
Write your child's description of each family member on the back!

Does your child know this personal information:
His/her whole name?
His/her street name?
His/her city and state?
Your **whole** name?
Where you work?

Day 7

WEEK

3

Physical Activity _____

Have your child cut with scissors on a line *(while you supervise).*
To help him/her with this activity, show your child how to put his/her thumb and first finger *together,* then apart, *together,* then apart.
Your child will use this same exercise when he/she uses the scissors.

Don't forget the pouring activity while your child is in the bath!

Parent—Did You Remember To

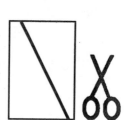

| HUG | READ TOGETHER | GIVE CHOICES | LISTEN | ASK QUESTIONS | PRAISE | HUG |

Mental Activity _____

"Today is **Sunday,** the **first** day of the week; a week has **7 days.**"
The color for the week is GREEN.

Have your child **find 3 green items** in the kitchen: *"The apron, bowl, and apple are green."*

Have your child **describe** each green item to you: *"Mom wears an apron to keep her clothes clean while she is cooking."* *"The small bowl is green."* *"I like to eat green Granny Smith apples."*

Today, using the 10–cup egg carton, practice matching "ONE TO ONE."

Match 1 cereal piece to each egg carton cup. **TOUCH and COUNT** with your child as each piece is placed. How many pieces are in the egg carton? Does your child think that he/she has **more** cereal in the egg carton or in the cereal box?

Day 1

WEEK

4

Another way to explain "ONE-TO-ONE" matching is at the dinner table.

Put plates on the table for dinner—4.

Have your child count the plates that you put on the table—4!

Then ask your child, **"Since** you counted 4 plates, **then** how many forks need to be on the dinner table?" Put 1 fork to the **left** of each plate. **"Since** there are 4 plates, **then** how many spoons need to be on the table?" Put 1 spoon to the **right** of each plate.

Physical Activity _____

The physical activity today will be to HEAR the difference in a clapping pattern.

Clap a 4- or 5-beat pattern for your child *(CLAP, CLAP, clap, clap, clap).*

Have your child repeat the pattern.

Make up several patterns. Let your child repeat each pattern.

Let your child make up some patterns for YOU.

Mental Activity _____

"Today is **Monday,** the **second** day of the week; a week has **7 days.**"

Have your child find green, this week's color, in a magazine, catalogue, or book.

Have your child **describe** the green item that was found: *"This is a picture of green grapes."*

Use the COUNTING BOX for a sequence activity.
Put 3 items on the table lined up *going away from your child.*
Which item is **first** or closest to him/her?
Which one is **last** or farthest away?
Which item is in the **middle?**
Which item is **biggest** or **smallest?**
Have your child **describe** the 3 items on the table by telling what each item is and what it is used for.

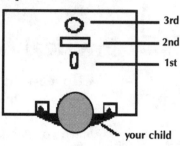

Day 2

WEEK

4

Your child will choose something green to wear tomorrow. He/she can choose a shirt, shorts, socks, a sweater, or even a ribbon.

Physical Activity _____

While outside, have your child hop over a stick.
With **both feet** facing the stick have him/her hop over the stick, then back.
With your child's **right foot** next to the stick have him/her hop over the stick and back on his/her **right foot.**
With your child's **left foot** next to the stick have him/her hop over the stick and back on his/her **left foot.**

Have your child continue to write/draw a line, a cross, a square, and a circle.

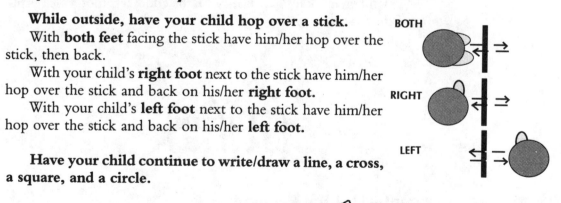

Continue pouring activity at bath time.

COUNTING BOX

BAG

Mental Activity

"Today is **Tuesday,** the **third** day of the week; a week has **7 days.**"
Today, get out the COUNTING BOX. You will use items from the box in a game called "Mystery Bag."

1. Put 1 item in a non-see-through bag. Let your child reach in and **describe** the item that he/she **feels.**
   (Is it round/square, light/heavy, rough/smooth, does make a sound/doesn't make a sound, etc?) Can your child guess what the item is?
2. Repeat the game several times.
3. Let your child put an item in the bag for YOU to describe.

Physical Activity

Clap a 5–beat pattern (*CLAP,* clap, *CLAP,* clap, *CLAP*).
Have your child **repeat the pattern** to you.
Create a new pattern.
Have your child repeat the pattern to you.

Have your child march to another room while you call out, "Left, right, left, right."

Watch your child. Is he/she using the correct foot with each direction?

Remember, mark his/her shoes with the code: **left** foot, black writing; **right** foot, red writing.

Parent—Did You Remember To

HUG   READ   GIVE   LISTEN   ASK   PRAISE   HUG
       TOGETHER   CHOICES   QUESTIONS

Mental Activity

"Today is **Wednesday,** the **fourth** day of the week; a week has **7 days.**"

Today, *using a shoestring,* your child **will thread 8 pasta pieces** (rigatoni or ziti).

Have your child Thread and Count as he/she threads each pasta piece. Take the pasta off the string.

Now have your child **string 9 pasta pieces.** Have your child **Thread and Count** while he/she strings each pasta piece. Take the pasta off the string.

Have your child **string 10 pasta pieces.** Have your child **Thread and Count** while he/she strings each pasta piece.

Tie the pasta string on your child's RIGHT wrist.

Ask your child to raise his/her **RIGHT** arm, then his/her **LEFT** arm. *(Remind your child that the bracelet is on his/her RIGHT wrist.)*

Ask your child to lift his/her **RIGHT** foot, then his/her **LEFT** foot.

Day 4
WEEK
4

Physical Activity

Roll a ball back and forth with your child.
Sit on the floor with your child about 4 feet away.
Roll the ball to your child.
Have your child roll the ball back to you.
Later, move farther apart and continue rolling the ball back and forth.
(This activity helps with your child's eye-hand coordination.)

Parent—Did You Remember To

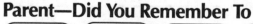

| HUG | READ TOGETHER | GIVE CHOICES | LISTEN | ASK QUESTIONS | PRAISE | HUG |

Mental Activity

"Today is **Thursday,** the **fifth** day of the week; a week has **7 days.**"

The color for the week is GREEN. Have your child find 3 green items in the yard. Name and describe each green item: *"The green hose is very long; we use it to get water to the flowers." "We use the green rake to clean up the leaves in the yard." "The green plant is on the table for decoration."*

Have your child follow these directions:

Go **through** the kitchen door, **around** the first chair, **under** the table, and **over** the second chair.

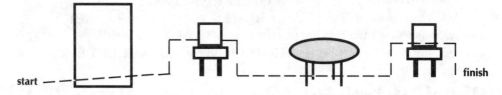

start   finish

Have your child touch all written labels in the kitchen and name each item.

Then have him/her **describe** each labeled item: *"A refrigerator is cold. Food is put into the refrigerator so that it will not spoil."*

If your child is not sure, tell him/her about the item: *"It is called a stove."*   *"We cook food on it."*   *"Everyone must be very careful around a stove because it gets very hot."*

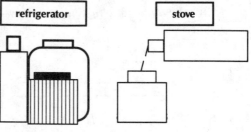

refrigerator   stove

Physical Activity

Write/draw a line, a cross, a square, and a circle.

Have your child hop
on his/her **right** foot 4 times.
on his/her **left** foot 3 times.

Continue the pouring activity at bath time.

Mental Activity

Remember to tell your child, "Today is **Friday,** the **sixth** day of the week; a week has **7 days.**"

Today, *after doing laundry,* **have your child sort through the laundry to find** the **category** of **socks** and the **category** of **T-shirts.**

TOUCH and **COUNT** both categories.

Which **category** had **more?** Which **category** had **less?**

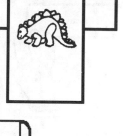

This week's color is green. Can your child find green among the laundry items?

Have your child set up categories in a dresser drawer—socks in one area, underwear in another area, and so on.

Which category had **most?**

Which category had **least?**

Day 6
WEEK
4

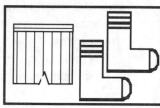

Physical Activity

While outside, practice BALL CATCHING and BALL THROWING with your child.

Remind your child to keep his/her eye on the **ball** when he/she is **catching.**

Remind your child to keep his/her eye on **you** when he/she is **throwing.**

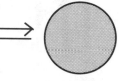

Today, make a **BOX FRONT PUZZLE** with your child.

Cut out the front of a box of cereal (or cake mix or whatever).

Then draw 4 or 5 lines on the back of the picture.

Your child will CUT WITH SCISSORS on the lines to create a new puzzle.

This activity should be done ONLY with your supervision!

Parent—Did You Remember To

HUG

READ TOGETHER

GIVE CHOICES

LISTEN

ASK QUESTIONS

PRAISE

HUG

Mental Activity

"Today is **Saturday,** the **seventh** day of the week; a week has **7 days.**"

Have your child practice identifying the labeled items in his/her bedroom *(bed, drawer, closet, etc.).*

While you point to the **label/word,** ask your child if he/she remembers what this **symbol** stands for. **If not, tell him/her again.**

After you wash the dishes, have your child sort the following into categories:

Forks. Have your child **dry** all forks, **count** them, and **put them away.** *(Your child has just collected a category of forks.)*

Spoons. Have your child **dry** all spoons, **count** them, and **put them away.** *(Your child has just collected a category of spoons.)*

Which category had **more?** Which category had **less?** Did both have the **same** number?

Day 7
WEEK
4

Physical Activity

While your child is outside, play a following directions game.
JUMP down a step with both feet.
RUN to the tree.
WALK heel-to-toe to the step.
Let your child give **you** 3 directions.
Continue the game with your child, taking turns and making up new directions each time.

Jump   **Run**   **Walk heel-to-toe**

Parent—Did You Remember To

HUG   **READ TOGETHER**   **GIVE CHOICES**   **LISTEN**   **ASK QUESTIONS**   **PRAISE**   **HUG**

Mental Activity _____

"Today is **Sunday,** the **first** day of the week; a week has **7 days.**"
(Repetition is the KEY TO LEARNING.)

ORANGE is the color for the week.

Find 3 orange items from a scarf drawer or jewelry box. **Describe**
the orange items: *"The butterfly has orange wings."* *"The pin has orange
beads."* *"The scarf has orange circles."*

Your child will LISTEN for the same beginning sounds.

Say to your child, "Zoo" and "Zap"; then ask your child if the
words **began (started) with the same sound.** Now repeat the following, but tell your child that *you are going to try to trick him/her.*

Do **rot** and **rip** have the same **beginning sound?**

Do **milk** and **monkey** have the same **beginning sound?**

Do *boot* and *apple* have the same **beginning sound?**

Continue the game: **eat** and **eagle? foot** and **feet?** *door* and *barn?*

rot and **rip**

boot and *apple*

Physical Activity _____

Have your child try to lace up his/her tennis shoes.

Show your child how to lace his/her shoe, and then let him/her try
this activity by himself/herself.

*Your child will probably have to practice this activity over and
over again!*

Your child should **choose his/her outfit for tomorrow—**
everything including shoes, socks, underwear, belt, and coat.

Parent—Did You Remember To

| HUG | READ TOGETHER | GIVE CHOICES | LISTEN | ASK QUESTIONS | PRAISE | HUG |

Mental Activity _____

1st time

2nd time

"Today is **Monday,** the **second** day of the week; a week has **7 days.**"

Use the 10-cup egg carton and minimarshmallows or cereal pieces.

Have your child count while placing **1** minimarshmallow into **each cup** of the egg carton. **How many** marshmallows were needed to fill up the egg carton?

Dump the 10 marshmallows from the egg carton onto the table.

Let your child **eat 2** marshmallows. Now have him/her **count again** while placing the marshmallows back into the egg carton. Ask, "How many marshmallows do you have?" Ask, "Do you now have **more** or **less** than the first time?"

Day 2

WEEK

5

Nest 3 items *(1 on top of the other, like boxes, bowls, or pans).*

Put the boxes out on the table and ask your child to put them together, biggest on the bottom to the smallest on the top.

After your child has finished, ask him/her, "Which is **biggest?**" "Which is **smallest?**" "Which is on the **top?**" "Which is on the **bottom?**" "Which is in the **middle?**"

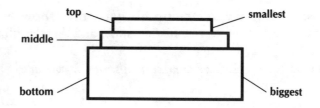

Physical Activity _____

Clap a 5–beat pattern for your child.
See if your child can **repeat the same pattern** to you.
Make up another 5-beat pattern for your child.
Could your child repeat that pattern to you?
Let your child make up a 5-beat clap pattern for **you!**
Have your child practice his/her writing/drawing with a line, a cross, a square, and a circle.

30

Mental Activity _____

"Today is **Tuesday,** the **third** day of the week; a week has **7 days.**"

The color for this week is ORANGE.

Find orange in a magazine. **Describe** the orange item: *"The two big balloons are orange."*

Play the BEGINNING SOUNDS game.

Have your child listen for **words that begin alike.** *Tell him/her that you are going to try to trick him/her!*

Do **hop** and **hat** have the same beginning sound? Do **sit** and **sap** have the same beginning sound? Do *dinosaur* and *fish* have the same beginning sound?

Continue the game: **cat** and **cake?** *man* and *coat?* **star** and **stop?** **rabbit** and **rat? wagon** and **water?** *yard* and *rain?*

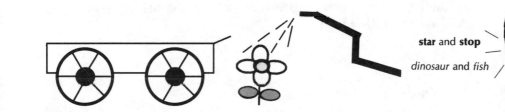

star and stop

dinosaur and fish

Physical Activity _____

Follow directions.

While outside, make up 3 directions for your child using the words *over, under, around, up,* and *down.*

For example:

Tell your child to step **over** the stick, crawl **under** the hose, and walk **around** the bike.

Then tell your child to walk **up** the step, walk **down** the step, and jump **over** the hose.

Make choices.

Your child needs to **choose his/her clothing for the next day.**

If your child cannot decide or makes an *inappropriate* choice, give him/her a **choice** between 2 outfits.

Mental Activity

"Today is **Wednesday,** the **fourth** day of the week; a week has **7 days.**"

Today, practice a **memory activity.**

Tell your child 4 numbers: *4, 6, 9, 1*

Ask your child to repeat the numbers to you: *4, 6, 9, 1*

If your child cannot remember 4 numbers, try 3 numbers.

Continue this memory activity using the numbers 1 through 9 only:

2, 5, 3, 6
9, 2, 4, 5
1, 6, 3, 2
3, 9, 1, 4

Physical Activity

Today, thread pasta (rigatoni or ziti) on a shoelace. Have your child do the following:

1. **Thread and Count 10** pieces.
2. Remove the pasta from the shoelace.
3. **Thread and Count 9** pieces of pasta.
   *Does he/she have **MORE** or **LESS** on the string than he/she had before?*
4. Remove the pasta from the shoelace.
5. **Thread and Count 8** pieces of pasta.
   *Does he/she have **MORE** or **LESS** than he/she had before?*

Tie the pasta string loosely on your child's RIGHT ankle.
Have your child climb **UP** a step with his/her **RIGHT** foot.
Have your child step **DOWN** the step on his/her **LEFT** foot.

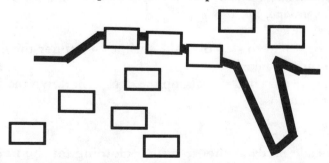

Have your child find the color orange in one of his/her library books.

Mental Activity _____

"Today is **Thursday,** the **fifth** day of the week; a week has **7 days.**"
Have your child practice the BEGINNING SOUNDS game.
Do **bag** and **beans** have the same beginning sound? Continue the game: **cat** and **cup?** *door* and *fish?* **lamp** and **lip? pan** and **pot?** *soup* and *rope?*

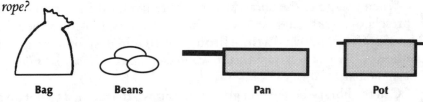

| Bag | Beans | Pan | Pot |

Physical Activity _____

Day 5
WEEK
5

Have your child FOLLOW these DIRECTIONS.
Have your child put his/her **RIGHT** hand on his/her **RIGHT** knee.
Have your child put his/her **LEFT** hand on his/her **LEFT** knee.
Have your child **HOP** 5 times on his/her **RIGHT** foot.
Have your child **HOP** 4 times on his/her **LEFT** foot.

Have your child write/draw a line, a cross, a square, and a circle.

Remember the pouring activity during bath time.

Pick out something ORANGE to wear tomorrow *(ribbon, shirt, socks).*

Parent—Did You Remember To

| HUG | READ TOGETHER | GIVE CHOICES | LISTEN | ASK QUESTIONS | PRAISE | HUG |

33

Mental Activity

"Today is **Friday, the sixth** day of the week; a week has **7 days.**"
Once a week take your child to the library.
Surround your child with books, and instill in your child the fact that books are important, wonderful things!

When you go to the library, ask the librarian for the location of the preschool books. Suggest to your child that he/she look on **1** shelf for **3 books.** Give your child a **time limit** (5 to 10 minutes) for picking out the books. *(In that way your child is learning to make decisions in a limited amount of time.)*

Call the library before you go to find out what is needed to obtain a library card.

Have your child find an example of the color orange while in the library.

Day 6

WEEK

5

Physical Activity

Play a game of CATCH outside with your child.

Throw the ball, *underhand,* to your child. Have your child throw back to you.

Remind your child to **watch the ball** when he/she is **trying to catch.**

And remind him/her to **watch the target/you** when he/she is **throwing to you.**

You are working on your child's eye-hand coordination.

Remind your child that he/she needs to keep his/her eye **on the target.** (The target is the **ball** or **you!**)

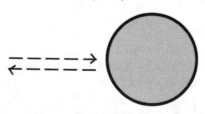

Make another BOX PUZZLE.
Draw 5 to 6 lines on the back of a box picture.
Let your **child cut on the lines while you supervise.**
Your child can spend some time putting his/her various BOX PUZZLES together.

You may need to put each puzzle together first to remind your child of the box picture.

Mental Activity _____

"Today is **Saturday,** the **seventh** day of the week; a week has **7 days.** Saturday is the **last** day of the week."

Let your child help you make a dessert (brownies, cookies, gelatin, a cake).

Read only 1 direction at a time to your child. Follow that 1 direction together with your child. Then move to the second direction and so on. Allow for messiness! Don't be in a hurry!

When finished, as a memory activity, ask your child to describe what was done **first, second,** and **third.**

While the cake is baking, play the BEGINNING SOUNDS game.

Do **cake** and **cot** begin with the same sound? Do *man* and *goat* begin with the same sound? Do **egg** and **elephant** begin with the same sound? Do **corn** and **cat** begin with the same sound? Do *sit* and *bat* begin with the same sound?

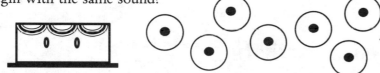

Physical Activity _____

Practice writing a line, a cross, a square, and a circle.

Play CATCH outside with your child using the handmade beanbag.

You might even set up a target *(box, old tire)* to throw the beanbag into!

Parent—Did You Remember To

HUG   READ TOGETHER   GIVE CHOICES   LISTEN   ASK QUESTIONS   PRAISE   HUG

Mental Activity

"Today is **Sunday,** the **first** day of the week; a week has **7 days.**"
The color of the week is PURPLE. Have your child find purple in a scarf drawer or jewelry box.

This week you and your child will study identification of SHAPES. Today's shape is a CIRCLE.
Ask your child if he/she can find any **circles** on the dinner table *(plates, glasses, cups, bowls).*
Draw a 5- or 6-inch circle on a piece of paper.
Let your child cut out the circle *with supervision.* Write the word *circle* on the cutout, and put it on your refrigerator.
Have your child look at these **circles.**
Which is **larger?** Which is **smaller?**
Color the circles purple.

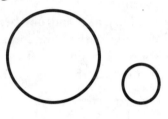

Physical Activity

Have your child practice writing the following numbers: 1, 2, 3, and 4.
Show your child how to make each number.
Remember, it will take your child a long time to control the muscles in his/her hand.
Is your child holding his/her pencil correctly?

Read a library book to your child.
(Point to each word as you read. You want your child to understand that these symbols stand for the words that you are reading.)

Parent—Did You Remember To

| HUG | READ TOGETHER | GIVE CHOICES | LISTEN | ASK QUESTIONS | PRAISE | HUG |

Mental Activity

"Today is **Monday,** the **second** day of the week; a week has **7 days.**"
Using 2 10-cup egg cartons, TOUCH and COUNT to 20.

Have your child put 1 bean **in** each cup of the first egg carton. Have him/her count as each bean is placed. Could your child count to 10 without any trouble?

If so, place a bean in each cup of the second egg carton, continuing to count from 11 to 20.

You may need to count together with your child from 11 to 20.

After all 20 beans have been placed, ask your child to count again by taking **out** the bean in each cup. Start in cup #1.

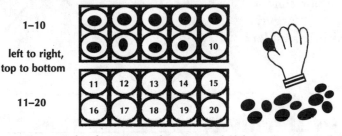

1–10

left to right,
top to bottom

11–20

Day 2
WEEK
6

Draw a 5- or 6-inch square; let your child cut it out (while you supervise).

Write the word *SQUARE* on the cutout, and put it on your refrigerator. Which of the squares to the right is **large?** Which is **small?**

Physical Activity

WRITE the numbers 1, 2, 3, 4, and 5 on a piece of paper.
Have your child practice **writing** each number.

Can your child **IDENTIFY/NAME** each number?

Have your child show you 1 lima bean, then 2 lima beans, then 3 lima beans, then 4 lima beans, then 5 lima beans, then 4 lima beans, then 3 lima beans, then 2 lima beans, then 1 lima bean.

Ask your child if he/she can remember the name of the SHAPE that he/she cut out yesterday.

If he/she does not remember, remind him/her that it was a **circle.**

Let your child identify red, yellow, blue, green, orange, and purple from the COUNTING BOX. *(Make sure all colors are represented in the box!)*

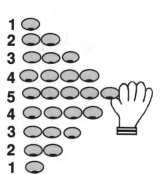

37

Mental Activity

"Today is **Tuesday,** the **third** day of the week; a week has **7 days.**"
The color for this week is PURPLE; find all purple items in the counting box.
TOUCH and COUNT.
DESCRIBE: "I found 5 purple milk bottle caps in the counting box."

The SHAPE for today is a TRIANGLE.
Draw a 5- or 6-inch triangle on a piece of paper. Have your child cut out the triangle *while you supervise.* Then write **TRIANGLE** on the shape, and put it on your refrigerator.
Ask your child to look at these triangles.
Which is **larger?**
Which is **smaller?**

Day 3
WEEK
6

Physical Activity

FOLLOW DIRECTIONS.
Have your child go **over** a stool, **under** the table, and **through** the kitchen door to **pick up** the pencil that is **on** the television.

Your child needs to pick out his/her clothing for the next day.
If your child cannot decide or makes an inappropriate choice, give him/her a choice between 2 outfits.

Have a beanbag toss outside. Have your child toss the bag into a box, over a clothesline, or at a target on the wall.

Parent—Did You Remember To

HUG

READ
TOGETHER

GIVE
CHOICES

LISTEN

ASK
QUESTIONS

PRAISE

HUG

Mental Activity _____

"Today is **Wednesday,** the **fourth** day of the week; a week has **7 days.**"

Have your child TOUCH and IDENTIFY the 3 shapes on the refrigerator (circle, square, and triangle).

Have your child **match** the shapes on this page by drawing a line from left to right.

Ask your child to tell you the **names** of these 3 shapes.

Have your child write the numerals 1, 2, 3, 4, and 5.

If you point to a number, can your child **identify/name** the number? Keep practicing number recognition with your child.

Ask your child to show you what:
3 cereal pieces look like

4 cereal pieces look like

5 cereal pieces look like

=3

=4

=5

Then what:
4 cereal pieces look like

3 cereal pieces look like

=4

=3

Day 4

WEEK

6

Can your child identify PURPLE from items in a sock drawer or jewelry box?

Sit with your child and read a library book.

Physical Activity _____

Let your child practice MATCHING ONE-TO-ONE at dinner.

For each plate, put
1 fork to the **left** of the plate.
1 spoon to the **right** of the plate.
1 cup/glass at the **top** of the spoon.
1 fruit to the **bottom** of the plate.

Remember, have your child place **1 item at a time** all the way around the table.

Mental Activity

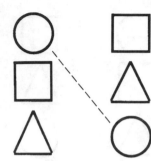

"Today is **Thursday,** the **fifth** day of the week; a week has **7 days.**"

Match the shapes on this page.

Can your child **NAME/IDENTIFY** these shapes?

WRITE the numbers 1, 2, 3, 4, and 5 on a piece of paper.

Have your child practice **writing** each number. Can your child **identify** each number? Have your child show you what

5 lima beans look like,
4 lima beans look like,
3 lima beans look like,
2 lima beans look like,
1 lima bean looks like.

Day 5

WEEK

6

Let your child identify red, yellow, blue, green, and purple items from a CRAYON BOX.

Physical Activity

Have your child FOLLOW DIRECTIONS.

Hop on **both** feet to the *faucet,*
Hop on your **left** foot to the *step,*
Hop on your **right** foot to the *tree.*

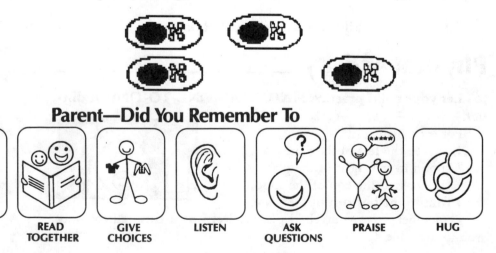

Parent—Did You Remember To

| HUG | READ TOGETHER | GIVE CHOICES | LISTEN | ASK QUESTIONS | PRAISE | HUG |

40

Mental Activity

"Today is **Friday**, the **sixth** day of the week; a week has **7 days**."

The color for the week is PURPLE.

Can your child find **purple** on a T-shirt?

Can your child match the LIKE/SAME shapes?

Have your child draw a line from left to right **matching** the shapes. Can your child **identify/name** the shapes?

Have your child practice drawing these shapes.

Use 2 10–cup egg cartons. Practice counting from 1 to 20.

Write the numbers 1 to 20 on the egg carton cups with a Magic Marker. You want your child to start associating the concept of **three** with the symbol **3**, the concept of **four** with the symbol **4**, and so on.

Have your child place 1 piece of popcorn per cup. Have him/her count out loud while placing the popcorn until he/she gets to 10. Then count **with** your child from 11 to 20.

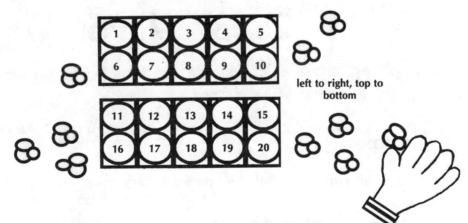

left to right, top to bottom

Physical Activity

Play catch with your child outside in the fresh air!

Ask your child to point to his/her ankle, wrist, heel, palm, calf, and waist.

Mental Activity

"Today is **Saturday,** the **seventh** day of the week; a week has **7 days.**"

Have your child TOUCH and IDENTIFY the 3 shapes on the refrigerator: circle, square, and triangle.

Can your child tell you the **names** of the 3 shapes? Can your child draw a circle and a square?

Does your child need help drawing a triangle?

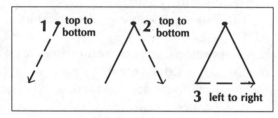

Show your child how to write the numerals 1, 2, 3, 4, 5, and 6.
Let your child practice **writing** each number.

Can your child **identify/name** each number? *If not, keep telling your child the **name** of the number symbol.*

Can your child identify a purple item from the COUNTING BOX?

Sit with your child and read a library book.

Day 7

WEEK

6

Physical Activity

Let your child MATCH ONE-TO-ONE at dinner.

For each plate, have your child put 1 piece of bread at the **bottom** of each plate all the way around the table.

Tell your child that he/she just matched 1 piece of bread to each plate.

Now, have your child match 1 potato to the top of each plate.

Mental Activity ─────────────────────

Tell your child, "Today is **Sunday,** the **first** day of the week; a week has **7 days.**"

This week's color will be BROWN.

Have your child find the color **brown** in his/her **bedroom.** How many brown items did he/she find? Have your child **describe** all brown items to you: *"The dresser has brown handles."*　*"The shorts are made of brown material."*

Have your child listen for same/alike ENDING sounds.

Ask your child to listen to each group of 3 words. Ask your child which **2** words **end** with the **same sound.**

hat	**rat**	*corn*
kitten	**mitten**	*pot*
boat	**corn**	**horn**
hand	**boot**	**toot**
farm	**charm**	*hen*

Play the What Is This Sound? game.

Have your child close his/her eyes, **listen,** and try to **name/identify** snapping fingers, opening a drawer, ringing a bell, wadding paper, knocking on the door, running water, and dropping coins.

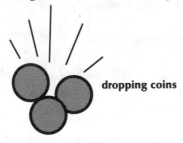

dropping coins

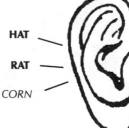

Day 1

WEEK

7

Physical Activity ─────────────────────

Can your child
balance on his/her **right** foot for 5 seconds? 10 seconds?
balance on his/her **left** foot for 5 seconds? 10 seconds?
raise his/her **right** hand? his/her **left** hand?
point to his/her **right** leg? his/her **left** leg?
point to his/her **right** wrist? his/her **left** wrist?
point to his/her **right** ankle? his/her **left** ankle?

Mental Activity _____

"Today is **Monday**, the **second** day of the week; a week has **7 days.**"

Use the COUNTING BOX. Put 3 items on the LEFT side of a table and 4 items on the RIGHT side of a table.

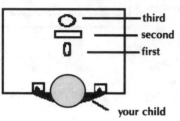

Have your child **TOUCH and COUNT** both groups.

Ask your child, "Which group has **more?** Which group of items has **less?**"

Now **line up** 3 items on the table *(going away from your child)*.

Ask your child, "Which item is **first** *(closest to child)?*" "Which item is **last** *(farthest from child)?*" "Which item is in the **middle?**"

Try this several times, changing the 3 items.

Stack up 3 books on the table, then ask your child, "Which book is on the **top?**" "Which book is on the **bottom?**" "Which book is in the **middle?**" "Which book is **first** *(top to bottom)?*" "Which book is **last?**"

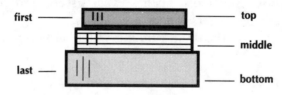

Can your child find the color BROWN on a shelf full of books?

Day 2
WEEK
7

Physical Activity _____

While outside, ask your child to jump forward and back 3 times.

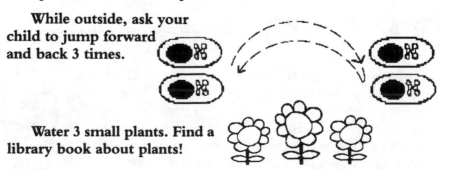

Water 3 small plants. Find a library book about plants!

44

Mental Activity _____

"Today is **Tuesday,** the **third** day of the week; a week has **7 days.**"
Have your child circle the 2 items that are ALIKE.

Have your child square the 1 item that is DIFFERENT.

Have your child match these numbers.

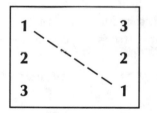

4	5
5	6
6	4

7	9
8	8
9	7

Physical Activity _____

Have your child practice writing 1 to 7.

^{1}▎1 ^{1}2 ^{1}3 ^{1}4 ^{3} ^{1}5 ^{3} ^{1}6 ^{1}7 ^{2}

Parent—Did You Remember To

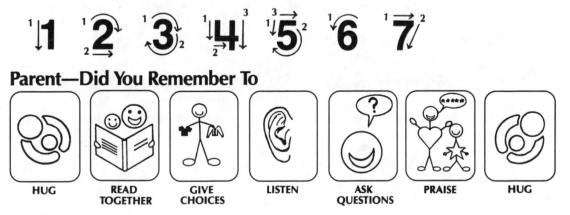

| HUG | READ TOGETHER | GIVE CHOICES | LISTEN | ASK QUESTIONS | PRAISE | HUG |

Mental Activity

"Today is **Wednesday,** the **fourth** day of the week; a week has **7 days.**"

Count to 20 with your child using the 2 10-cup egg cartons. TOUCH and COUNT with raisins or grapes or nuts.

left to right,

top to bottom

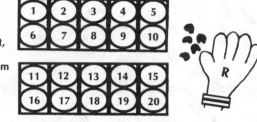

Have your child help you make Jell-O.

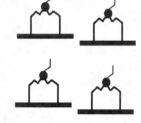

Day 4

WEEK

7

1. With your child read and follow **1 direction at a time.**
2. **You will need to measure the hot water and put it into the bowl.**
3. Your child can measure the cold water and put it into the Jell-O mixture. Let him/her stir the mixture.
4. Let your child help you put the Jell-O mixture into the mold or molds. (Don't forget to add the fruit or nuts from the counting exercise.)
5. After finishing, ask your child to tell you what was done **first, second,** and **third.**

Have your child circle the 2 items that are ALIKE.
Have your child square the 1 item that is DIFFERENT.

Physical Activity

Have your child practice writing the numbers 1 to 8.

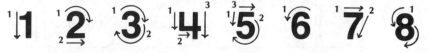

Play beanbag catch with your child.

Mental Activity

"Today is **Thursday,** the **fifth** day of the week; a week has **7 days.**"
Ask your child to describe 3 items: a fork, a chair, and a bowl *(whatever!).*

Ask the following questions in order to help your child understand what descriptive words are and how they are used: "What is the **name** of the item?" "How is it **used?**" "What **color** is it?" "What is it **made of?**" "Is it **short? long?**" "Is it **soft? hard?**" "Is it **light? heavy?**" "Is it **little? big?**" "Is it **round? square?**"

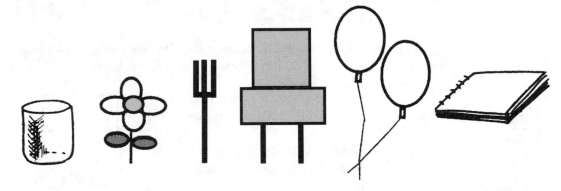

Physical Activity

Find categories from the COUNTING BOX.
Pick out the category of **red** items *(barrettes, pencils, balloons).* **TOUCH and COUNT.**
Pick out the category of **round** items *(milk caps).* **TOUCH and COUNT.**
Pick out the category of **writing** tools *(pencils, pens, crayons).* **TOUCH and COUNT.**

COUNTING BOX

Practice writing a line, a cross, a square, a circle, and a triangle. Practice numbers, too!

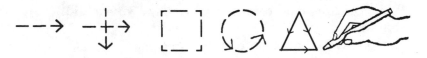

Have your child practice jumping over a rope.
Have 2 people hold a rope about 2″ high.
Facing the rope, your child should jump over the rope. Can he/she jump over on his/her **right** foot? on his/her **left** foot?

Mental Activity _____

"Today is **Friday,** the **sixth** day of the week; a week has **7 days.**"
Cut a carrot into 20 pieces.
Use the carrot slices to **TOUCH and COUNT** to 20.

left to right,

top to bottom

The color for the week is brown; find brown outside: *"The tree bark is brown."*   *"The football is brown."*   *"The skateboard is brown."*

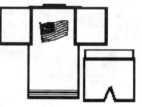

Have your child sort his/her laundry into the categories of socks, shorts, underwear, T-shirts.
TOUCH and COUNT each category.
Which category has the **most?** Which category has the **least?**

Physical Activity _____

Make a box puzzle.
Use any kind of box front.
Draw 3 to 5 lines on the back.
Let your child cut on the lines with scissors *(always supervise your child while he/she uses scissors).*
Practice putting together collected **cereal box puzzles.**
If your child does not remember the picture, put the puzzle together for him/her.
Let your child look at the picture for 5 seconds; then mix up the puzzle pieces and let your child put the puzzle together.

While outside, read these 3 directions to your child.
Run to the tree.
Creep/crawl *on all fours* around the tree.
Skip back to the starting point!

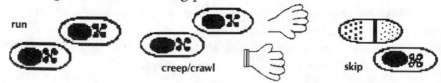

run

creep/crawl   skip

Mental Activity _____

"Today is **Saturday,** the **seventh** day of the week; a week has **7 days**. This is the **last** day of the week."

Check to see if your child knows this personal information:
His/her entire name
Home address
Home phone number
Your entire name
Where you work

Mrs. Susan James

Mr. Thomas James

The color of the week is BROWN. Have your child find something brown in the kitchen.

Physical Activity _____

Roll a ball to your child.
Have your child **kick** the ball with his/her **right** foot.
Have your child **kick** the ball with his/her **left** foot.

Have your child throw a ball into a box
from 2 feet away.
from 3 feet away.

Day 7

WEEK

7

Make up a following directions game using these words: *in, out, through, around, up, and down.*

Parent—Did You Remember To

HUG

READ TOGETHER

GIVE CHOICES

LISTEN

ASK QUESTIONS

PRAISE

HUG

Mental Activity

COUNTING BOX

"Today is **Sunday,** the **first** day of the week; a week has **7 days.**"
Play a memory game with your child.

Take 3 items from the counting box and put them on the table. Let your child look at the items for 5 seconds. Now put the items back into the box.

Can your child find the **same** 3 items in the counting box?

Then can your child put them back on the table in the **same order?**

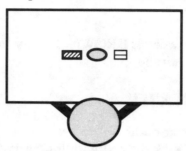

The color for the week is WHITE. Can your child find white in the kitchen? *"The stove is white."*   *"The table has white paint."*
"The towel has white flowers."

Physical Activity

Have your child practice writing.

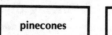

Turn to page 81 in the back of the book. It is a calendar for your refrigerator. Each day write in the day of the week.

While outside have your child find two categories *(pinecones, pebbles).*

pinecones	pebbles

Day 1

WEEK

8

Parent—Did You Remember To

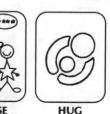

HUG   READ TOGETHER   GIVE CHOICES   LISTEN   ASK QUESTIONS   PRAISE   HUG

Mental Activity

"Today is **Monday,** the **second** day of the week; a week has **7 days.**"

The color for the week is WHITE.

Point to a **white** triangle on this page.

Have your child point to: the **small** circle, the **large** circle, the **big** square, the **little** square, the **lesser** triangle, the **greater** triangle.

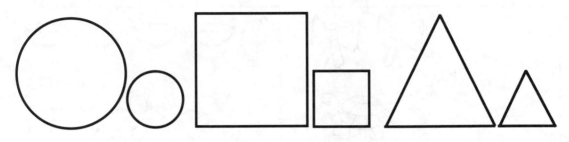

Ask your child to find something white in the kitchen.
Have him/her **describe** the item to you. *"The cookie jar is white."*

Count out loud to 20.

Physical Activity

Turn to pages 83 and 85.
Have your child identify and color all shapes.

Day 2

WEEK

8

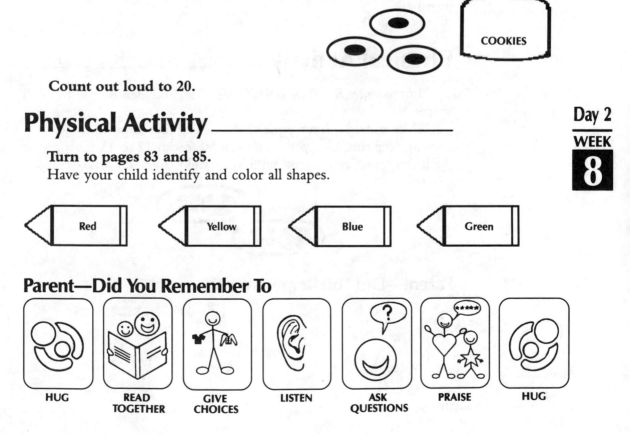

Red	Yellow	Blue	Green

Parent—Did You Remember To

| HUG | READ TOGETHER | GIVE CHOICES | LISTEN | ASK QUESTIONS | PRAISE | HUG |

Mental Activity _____

"Today is **Tuesday,** the **third** day of the week; a week has **7 days.**"
The color for the week is WHITE. Have your child find white in a book or magazine. *"The pages are white."*

Have your child match the numbers with the correct group of items.

Count out loud together with your child to 20.
Point to each number. Can your child identify/name each number?

6   3   5   2   1   4

Physical Activity _____

Turn to pages 87, 89, and 91. Have your child identify and color all shapes.
While outside, have your child run 90 feet *(approximately).*
Time the run. Can your child run 90 feet in 12 to 15 seconds?
If not, practice running with your child *(every day or so, for a few minutes).*

Day 3

WEEK

8

Parent—Did You Remember To

HUG   READ   GIVE   LISTEN   ASK   PRAISE   HUG
TOGETHER   CHOICES   QUESTIONS

Mental Activity

"Today is **Wednesday,** the **fourth** day of the week; a week has **7 days.**"

The color for the week is **WHITE. Have your child find white outside.** *"The sidewalk is white."*

Have your child match the numbers with the correct group of items.

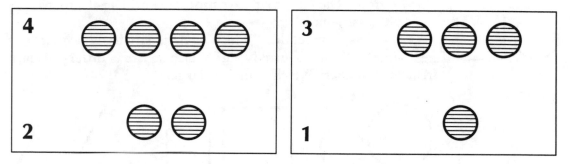

Physical Activity

Glue pages 83, 85, 87, 89, and 91 to cardboard.
Parent, cut out the shapes that your child has colored.
Can your child identify each shape?
Can your child name each color?

Day 4

WEEK

8

Parent—Did You Remember To

| HUG | READ TOGETHER | GIVE CHOICES | LISTEN | ASK QUESTIONS | PRAISE | HUG |

Mental Activity

"Today is **Thursday**, the **fifth** day of the week; a week has **7 days.**"

The color for the week is WHITE. Have your child find white in the closet. *"The towel is white."* *"The sheets have white flowers."*

Using the red, blue, and yellow cutout shapes, ask your child to sort into groups of **circles, squares,** and **triangles.**

TOUCH and COUNT each group. How many were in each group? Did one group have **more? fewer?** Did all groups have the **same** number?

Ask your child: "Which circle is **small?** Which circle is **large?**" "Which square is **big?** Which square is **little?**" "Which triangle is **smaller?** Which triangle is **larger?**"

Have your child match the numbers with the correct group of items.

Day 5	
WEEK 8	

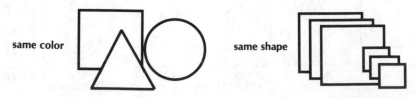

Physical Activity

Parent, cut out the shapes that your child has colored. Ask your child to **match:**

as to **color** *(all yellow together, all red together, etc.).*

as to **shape** *(all circles together, all squares together, etc.).*

same color   same shape

Mental Activity _____

"Today is **Friday,** the **sixth** day of the week; a week has **7 days.**"
Have your child **match the alphabet letters in each box.** *Draw a line from left to right.*

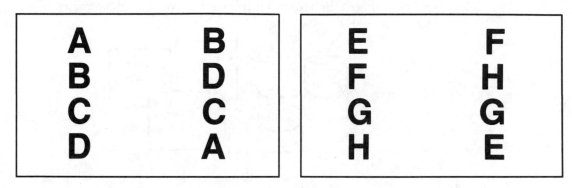

Have your child **match the number to the correct amount.** *Draw a line from left to right.*

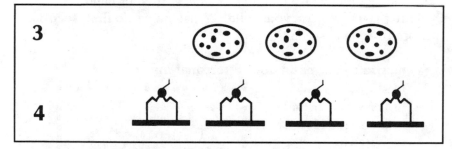

Day 6

WEEK

8

After matching numbers to pictures, have your child show you what 5 lima beans look like, what 6 lima beans look like, 7, 8, 9, and 10!

Physical Activity _____

Have your child **bounce a ball** *8 times, 7 times, 6 times, 5 times, 4 times, 3 times, 2 times, 1 time.*

Parent—Did You Remember To

| HUG | READ TOGETHER | GIVE CHOICES | LISTEN | ASK QUESTIONS | PRAISE | HUG |

55

Mental Activity

"Today is **Saturday,** the **last** day of the week, the **seventh** day."

Today, let your child help you sort groceries into the **category** of **cans.** How many cans are there? the **category** of **boxes.** How many boxes are there? the **category** of **plastic bottles.** How many plastic bottles are there?

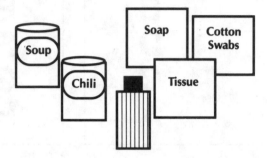

Make pudding with your child.
Read and follow 1 direction at a time with your child.
After you finish, ask your child, "What did we do **first, second** (or next), **third?"** and so on.

Question your child about personal information.
Does he/she know
His/her whole name?
His/her street address?
City? State?
Your whole name?
Where you work?

Billy James
411 Maple Street
Atlanta, Georgia
Susan & Bob James
Maple Computers

Day 7

WEEK

8

Physical Activity

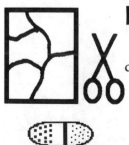

Make a new BOX PUZZLE (with a cereal box, brownie box, cake mix box).

Can your child find **white** on the box puzzle?

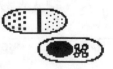

Show your child how to skip.
Have your child skip from the step to the sidewalk.
This skill may take a bit of practice. Have your child keep trying.

Mental Activity

"Today is **Sunday,** the **first** day of the week; a week has **7 days.**"
While in the kitchen, play a game of RHYMING WORDS.
Say to your child, "Listen to these 3 words. Which 2 rhyme?"

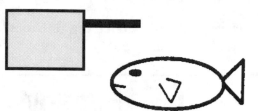

1. **pot, hot,** sat
2. **cable,** red, **table**
3. **fish, dish,** line
4. **cat,** water, **hat**
5. dish, **stair, chair**

    **The color for the week is BLACK. Can your child find black
on this page?** *"The print on the page is black."* **Remember to write in
the day of the week on your refrigerator calendar!**

Physical Activity

Have your child play TRASH CAN BASKETBALL.
See if your child can **sink** a ball (beanbag) in an empty trash can
while standing 3 feet away.

Have your child practice writing numbers and drawing shapes.

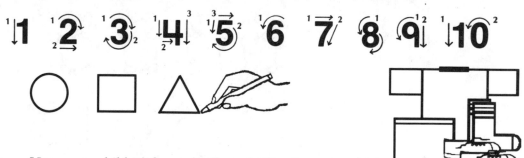

Have your child **pick out his/her clothes for tomorrow.**
Your child should **continue the pouring activity at bath time.**

Day 1
WEEK
9

Parent—Did You Remember To

 HUG   READ TOGETHER   GIVE CHOICES   LISTEN   ASK QUESTIONS   PRAISE   HUG

Mental Activity

Refer to the weekly calendar. Ask your child, "Can you remember the **name** of this day of the week?"

Write in **Monday.** Ask your child if he/she can tell you today's **name.**

Have your child match the alphabet letters in each box. *Draw a line from left to right.*

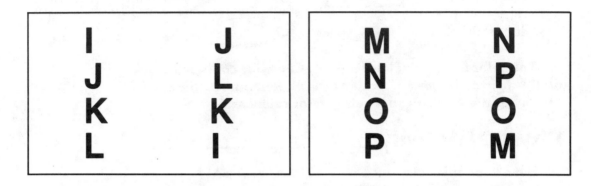

Have your child match the number to the correct amount. *Draw a line from left to right.*

After matching numbers to pictures, have your child show you what 10 lima beans look like, 9, 8, 7, 6, 5, 4, and 3.

Day 2

WEEK

9

Physical Activity

Have your child walk a 4-foot line *(crack in sidewalk)* **heel-to-toe. How many steps did he/she take?**

Mental Activity —————————————

Refer to the weekly calendar. Ask your child, "What is the **name** of this day of the week?"

You need to write in **Tuesday.** Ask your child to try to name the days of the week in **sequence.**

The color of the week is black. Can your child find black on a magazine page?

Have your child **describe** the **black** item: "The print on the magazine page is **black.**" "The sports car is **black.**"

It is RHYMING WEEK. This time, find words that rhyme with items in your living room.

Point to the **table,** and ask your child its **name.** Then say, "Does **cable** rhyme with **table?**"

Point to the **chair;** ask your child its **name.** Then say, "Does **fair** rhyme with **chair?**"

Point to the **rug;** ask your child its **name.** Then say, "Does *pot* rhyme with *rug?*"

Continue the game: **door** and **floor?** *couch* and *lamp?*

Have your child use 2 10-cup egg cartons for counting.

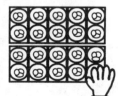

1. Have your child **TOUCH and COUNT** to 20. *Use popcorn or cereal for counting pieces.*
2. Now have your child **eat the popcorn in cup #20,** then dump the popcorn on the table.
3. **TOUCH and COUNT** *again.* How many pieces are left in the counting cartons?
4. Have your child **eat the popcorn in cup #19.** Dump the popcorn on the table.
5. **TOUCH and COUNT** *again.* How many pieces are left in the counting cartons?
6. Every time your child eats a piece of popcorn, does he/she have **more** or **less** in the cartons?

Day 3

WEEK

9

Physical Activity —————————————

Let your child pour the drinks for dinner.

Have your child **match 1 drink** to each **plate.**

(**No hot drinks,** *and be sure to use nonbreakable cups and glasses in this activity.*)

Mental Activity

Refer to the weekly calendar. Ask your child, "What is the **name** of this day of the week?"

You, the parent, need to write in Wednesday. Ask your child if he/she can name the days of the week in sequence.

It is RHYMING WEEK. Find words today that rhyme with items found in the bedroom.

Point to the **bed,** and ask your child its **name.** Then say, "Does **bed** rhyme with **red?**"

Point to the **lamp;** ask your child its **name.** Then say, "Does **lamp** rhyme with **camp?**"

Point to the **rug;** ask your child its **name.** Then say, "Does *rat* rhyme with *rug?*"

Continue the game: **door** and **floor?** *sheet* and *pants?*

Circle the two letters in each box that are ALIKE.

A B A	D D B
F E F	**C G C**

Physical Activity

Have your child follow these directions:
Creep/crawl from the *living room* to the *kitchen.*
Stand up and **hop** back to the *living room.*
Climb over the *stool.*

Your child should be making clothing choices each night for the next day. Give him/her a time limit.

Make it a game. Give your child 5 to 10 minutes to pick out tomorrow's clothing.

If he/she doesn't pick out something in 5 to 10 minutes, **you** get to pick out his/her clothing for tomorrow.

Use a kitchen timer!

Mental Activity

Refer to the weekly **calendar.** Ask your child, "What is the **name** of this day of the week?"

You, the parent, need to write in **Thursday.** Ask your child to tell you the **name** of the days of the week in order.

Circle the alphabet letter that is DIFFERENT.

Have your child try to count out loud to 20.

Physical Activity

Make up a 5-beat clapping sequence. Can your child repeat the same sequence to you?

Let your child make up a clapping sequence for **YOU** to repeat.

While playing outside, have your child follow directions using these words:

up, down, around, through, in, and *out.*

Read together with your child.

Let your child pick the book. Point to each word as you read.

Day 5

WEEK

9

Parent—Did You Remember To

HUG   READ TOGETHER   GIVE CHOICES   LISTEN   ASK QUESTIONS   PRAISE   HUG

Mental Activity _____

Refer to the weekly **calendar.** Ask your child, "What is the **name** of this day of the week?"

You, the parent, need to write in **Friday.** Can your child tell you the **name** of each day of the week in order?

Using the 2 10-cup egg cartons, have your child TOUCH and COUNT to 20.

Have your child match the alphabet letters in each box.

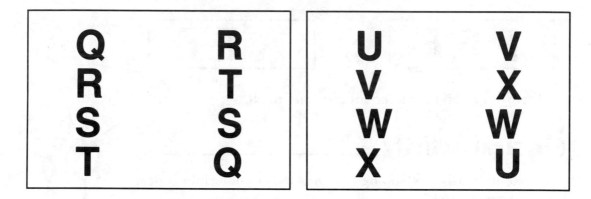

Physical Activity _____

Have your child fix the plates for a meal, placing one item at a time. *Make sure that your child is scooping from plastic bowls, **not hot pots!***
Use any or all of the following. Allow for some messiness!

One piece of fruit for each plate
One green vegetable for each plate
One yellow vegetable for each plate
One slice of meat for each plate
One piece of bread for each plate
One drink for each plate

Your child has just matched each item **ONE-TO-ONE** (one item to one plate).

While playing outside, have your child use a ball to explain the following words: *over, under, between.*
*He/she can throw the ball **over** the bush. He/she can throw the ball **under** the swing. He/she can throw the ball **between** the trees.*

Day 6

WEEK

9

Mental Activity _____

Refer to the weekly **calendar.** Ask your child, "What is the **name** of this day of the week?"

You, the parent, need to write in **Saturday.** Ask your child to say the name of the days of the week in sequence.

Review your child's personal information knowledge. Does he/she know his/her whole **name?** his/her home **address? city? state?** his/her home **phone number? your** whole **name?** where **you work?**

Have your child match these alphabet letters.

X	Z
Y	Y
Z	X

M	N
V	M
N	V

SUZY McDONALD
940 OAK STREET
ALBANY, NEW YORK
JOAN McDONALD
ACME PRINTING

TOMMY SMITH
244 CENTER STREET
ALBANY, NEW YORK
SUE & TOM SMITH
CORNER GROCERY

Physical Activity _____

Play ball outside: catch and throw, roll and kick! Skip with your child down the driveway or sidewalk.

Parent—Did You Remember To

HUG   READ   GIVE   LISTEN   ASK   PRAISE   HUG
         TOGETHER   CHOICES   QUESTIONS

Mental Activity

Today is **Sunday.**
Play a memory game with your child.

1. Put 3 crayons on the table *(red, yellow, and blue)*.
2. Let your child look at the 3 colors for 5 seconds.
3. Put the 3 crayons back into the crayon box.
4. Have your child pick out the **same 3 crayons** and place them on the table.

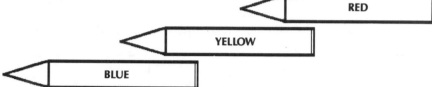

RED

YELLOW

BLUE

Play the BEGINNING SOUNDS game.

Do **bone** and **bow** begin with the same sound? **Say to your child, "Don't let me trick you!"** Do *corn* and *born* begin with the same sound? Do **pig** and **pot** begin with the same sound? Do *hop* and *top* begin with the same sound? Do **tie** and **top** begin with the same sound?

Physical Activity

Show your child how to **walk backward** on a cement sidewalk crack *(4 or 5 feet)*.

Count out loud while you are taking the steps.

THEN have your child **walk backward** *(toe-to-heel)* over the same distance.

Count out loud while he/she is taking the steps.

Who took **more** steps? Who took **fewer** steps? **Why?**

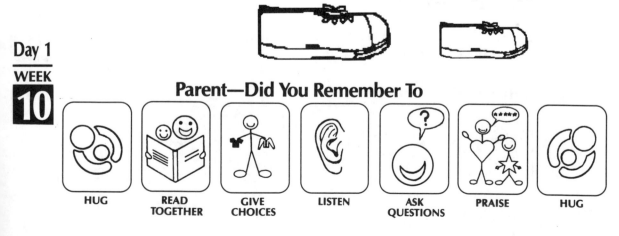

Day 1

WEEK

10

Parent—Did You Remember To

HUG

READ
TOGETHER

GIVE
CHOICES

LISTEN

ASK
QUESTIONS

PRAISE

HUG

Mental Activity

Write in **Monday** on the calendar.

Today, use the green, orange, and purple CutOut Shapes from the COUNTING BOX.

Then have your child **sort** shapes into these groups:

Green shapes
Orange shapes
Purple shapes

Can your child **identify** each **color?**

Next have your child **sort** the CutOut Shapes into these groups:

Circles
Squares
Triangles

Can your child **identify** each **shape?**

Using the **group of circles,** have your child point to

the **larger** green circle.
the **bigger** orange circle.
the **greater** purple circle.
the **small** green circle.
the **little** orange circle.
the **lesser** purple circle.

all green shapes		all purple shapes
	all orange shapes	

all circles		all squares
	all triangles	

G	O	P
G	O	P
Green	Orange	Purple

Count out loud with your child to 20. Can your child name/identify the numbers from 1 to 10?

1   2   3   4   5   6   7   8   9   10

Physical Activity

While outside, draw a circle in the dirt or on the sidewalk. Ask your child to: Stand **outside** the circle.
Stand **inside** the circle.
Stand **on** the circle.

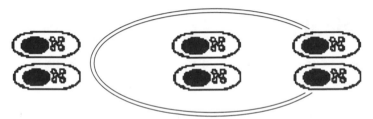

Have your child run 90 feet. Can he/she run it in 12 seconds?

Mental Activity

Ask your child the **name** of the day of the week. Write in **Tuesday** on your calendar.

left to right, top to bottom

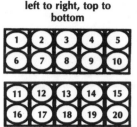

Have your child **TOUCH and COUNT to 20.**

Using celery pieces, match 1 celery piece to each of the 20 egg cups. Have your child count as he/she places each celery piece *(you may need to help him/her count to 20).*

NOW pour the 20 celery pieces on the table. You and your child may **eat 1 piece each.**

Let your child **TOUCH and COUNT** the remaining celery pieces. HOW MANY WERE LEFT?

Let your child help **dry utensils** after a meal.

Have your child **SORT** utensils into categories (no knives!)—all forks, all spoons.

How many were in each category? Which group had **more?** Which group had **less?**

Can your child NAME all the items in his/her bedroom (bed, dresser, closet, lamp, table, pillow)?

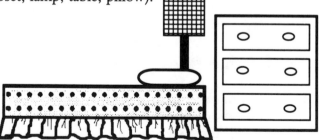

Day 3

WEEK

10

Physical Activity

Have your child help clean up the yard. Your child can rake or sweep off the patio. Do any plants need repotting?

Remember to have your child **pick out his/her clothes for the next day.** *Give a time limit.*

Mental Activity _____

It's **Wednesday. Write in the name of the day of the week on the calendar.**

Have your child stack 3 towels.
Ask him/her, "Which towel is on **top**?"
Ask, "Which towel is on the **bottom**?"
Ask, "Which towel is **between** the other 2?"
Can your child tell you the **color names** of each towel?

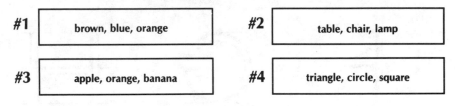

Ask your child to repeat the words in box #1 after you *in the same order.* Continue the same routine with boxes #2, #3, and #4.

#1 | brown, blue, orange | **#2** | table, chair, lamp

#3 | apple, orange, banana | **#4** | triangle, circle, square

Physical Activity _____

Have your child bounce a ball 10 times.
Roll a ball back and forth with your child 20 times.
Roll a ball to your child so that he/she can kick the ball with his/her RIGHT foot.
Roll a ball to your child so that he/she can kick the ball with his/her LEFT foot.

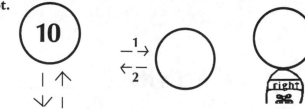

Day 4

WEEK

10

Parent—Did You Remember To

HUG | READ TOGETHER | GIVE CHOICES | LISTEN | ASK QUESTIONS | PRAISE | HUG

Mental Activity

Write in the day on the calendar. It's Thursday.

Use this page as a reference on how to make the capital letters of the alphabet.

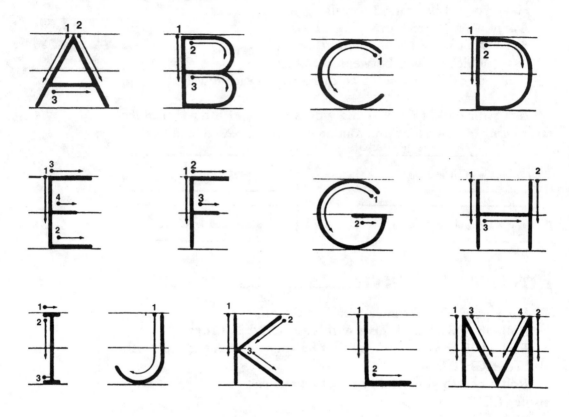

Physical Activity

Have your child practice making 1 letter each day. When you finish all 26 letters, start over!

Have your child TOUCH and COUNT each letter on this page. How many letters are on this page?

While outside, have your child hop 6 times on 2 feet, hop 6 times on his/her right foot, and hop 6 times on his/her left foot.

Mental Activity _____

It's **Friday.** Does your child know the name of this day of the week?

Match the number symbol to the appropriate number of objects.

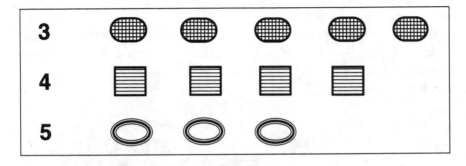

Put 3 items on the table (*going away from your child*).

Which item is in **first** place? Which item is in **third/last** place? Which item is in **second/middle** place?

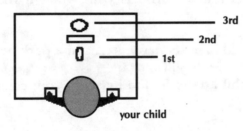

Sort groceries looking for paper products.

Your child needs to identify the **category** of paper products. **TOUCH and COUNT** the paper items.

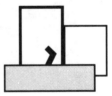

From the CutOut Shapes, **check to see if your child can identify the following colors:** red, yellow, blue, green, orange, purple.

Physical Activity _____

Ask your child to set the table. Give him/her 3 directions:

Put 4 **bowls** on the table.

We also need 4 **spoons** and 4 **napkins.**

Mental Activity _____

It's the **last** day of the week, the **seventh** day. Does your child know the **name** of this day of the week?

Ask your child the following:

"If you have 2 children and 1 bicycle, can you **match** 1 bicycle to each child?" "Then how many children would be able to ride the bike? How many would **not?**"

"If you have 2 children and 2 skateboards, can you **match** each child to a skateboard?" "How many children **would** have a skateboard?" "Would there be any children who **would not** have a skateboard?"

Go over PERSONAL INFORMATION.

Does your child know his/her whole **name?** his/her **address? city? state?** his/her **phone number? your** whole **name?** where **you work?**

Can your child identify/name items in a park or yard: swing, tree, path, dog, flower, and plant?

Have your child describe the items to you: color, size, shape, and use.

The big tree has brown bark and green leaves.
The swing is made of rope and a wooden board.
We use the swing to "fly" back and forth.
The flower is pink and smells sweet.

Day 7

WEEK

10

Physical Activity _____

Play outside: ride a bike, skate, or try out a skateboard!

Mental Activity

This is **Sunday.**

Using the CutOut Shapes from the counting box, have your child **identify** the **colors:** red, yellow, blue, green, orange, and purple. Also, have your child **identify** the **shapes:** circle, square, and triangle.

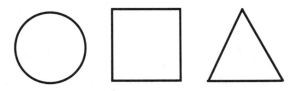

Using the CutOut Shapes again, put **4 colors** on the table. While your child covers his/her eyes, take 1 color away. Ask your child **which color is missing.**

TOUCH and COUNT to 20 using popcorn/carrot pieces and 2 10-cup egg cartons.

left to right, top to bottom

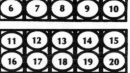

1. Have your child place 1 piece of popcorn/carrot per cup until he/she counts to 20.
2. Then have your child **spill** the 20 pieces from the egg cartons onto the table.
3. Let your child eat 1 piece of the popcorn/carrot.
4. Then have your child **TOUCH and COUNT** again. How many popcorn/carrot pieces does he/she have left?
5. Spill the contents on the table again. Let your child eat 1 more piece of popcorn/carrot.
6. Have your child **TOUCH and COUNT.** How many pieces were left? Does your child keep having **more** or **less?**

Physical Activity

Play catch and throw with your child; use the beanbag.

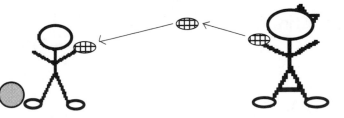

Bounce a ball *(with 2 hands)* **5 times, 6 times, 7 times, and 8 times.**

Day 1

WEEK

11

Mental Activity

"It's **Monday**. It's the **second** day of the week. Write **Monday** on the calendar."

Color the first circle red, the second yellow, the third blue, the fourth green, the fifth orange, and the sixth purple.

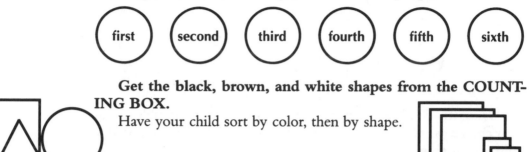

Get the black, brown, and white shapes from the COUNT-ING BOX.

Have your child sort by color, then by shape.

same color

same shape

Physical Activity

Put a book under the kitchen table.

Have your child follow these directions:

Go to the kitchen, look under the table, and bring me the object there.

Read the book to your child. Point to each word as you read.

Ask your child:

Who/what was the book about?

What happened in the story?

Did you like the story? Why? Why not?

Did you learn anything from the story?

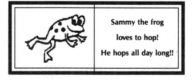

Sammy the frog
loves to hop!
He hops all day long!!

Parent—Did You Remember To

Day 2

WEEK

11

HUG

READ
TOGETHER

GIVE
CHOICES

LISTEN

ASK
QUESTIONS

PRAISE

HUG

Mental Activity _____

Write in **Tuesday** on the calendar.

From the COUNTING BOX sort all SOLID COLOR items into color groups (all red together, all blue together, etc.).

Then ask your child which **category** or group of things has the **most.** Which category or group has the **least?** Did all categories have the **same** number? Have your child **TOUCH and COUNT** to find out!

Is there **another way** to **sort** the items in the **COUNTING BOX?** Maybe the categories could be milk bottle caps, barrettes, and thread spools. Which category has the **most?** Which category has the **least?**

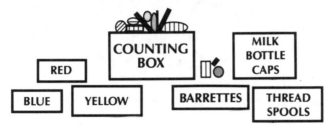

Point to labeled items in the living room. Have your child name/identify the items.

Can your child **describe** each item?
What does it do? What color is it?
What material is it made of?

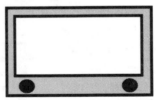

Physical Activity _____

Give your child these 4 directions:
Touch your toes.
Clap your hands behind your back.
Pat your head.
Clap your hands.

Parent—Did You Remember To

HUG

READ
TOGETHER

GIVE
CHOICES

LISTEN

ASK
QUESTIONS

PRAISE

HUG

Day 3
WEEK
11

Mental Activity _____

Today is **Wednesday.** Write it on your calendar!
Have your child match (*draw a line top to bottom*) **one happy face to one apple.**

Was there one apple for each person? Were there any apples left? How many?

Play the BEGINNING SOUNDS game. Do these words begin with like/similar sounds?

pot and **pat**
jump and **jack**
red and *late*
mat and *nat*
cake and **cat**

Use the 2 10-cup egg cartons to have your child TOUCH and COUNT to 20 using popcorn, dried beans, or celery pieces. Then see if your child can count out loud to 20 by himself/herself.

Physical Activity _____

Have your child **play outside every day** *any kind of ball game.* It helps his/her eye-hand coordination.

Day 4
WEEK
11

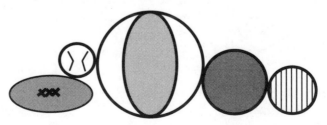

74

Mental Activity _____

Write in the day on your calendar. It's Thursday.

Use this page as a reference on how to make the capital letters of the alphabet.

Have your child practice making 1 letter each day. When you finish all 26 letters, start over!

Have your child TOUCH and COUNT each letter on this page. How many letters are on this page?

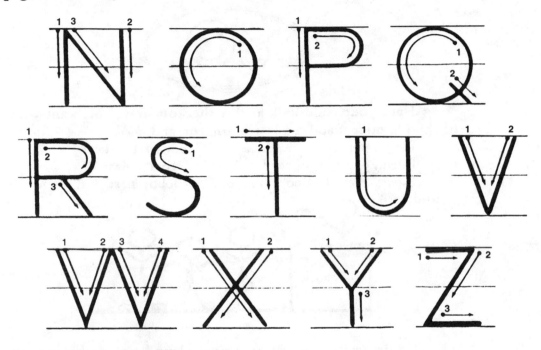

Physical Activity _____

Pick out flower seeds with your child. Read together and follow the planting directions.

Give your child the **task** of watering the plant every day!

Parent—Did You Remember To

| HUG | READ TOGETHER | GIVE CHOICES | LISTEN | ASK QUESTIONS | PRAISE | HUG |

Day 5
WEEK
11

75

Mental Activity _____

Write in **Friday** on the calendar.

After your child has seen a movie or a TV program, ask him/ her fact questions about the story: "**Who** was the main character?" "**What** was he/she doing?" "**When** did this story take place?" "**Where** did this happen?" "**Why** did he/she _____?"

Use the 5 words *who, what, when, where,* and *why* when you want to question your child about **STORY FACTS.**

Have your child look at this checkout line. You want your child to understand the words *first, last,* **and** *middle.*

Parent, point to Jenny and ask, "Is Jenny **first** or **last?**"

Parent, point to Sam and ask, "Is Sam **first** or **last?**"

Parent, point to Bobby and ask, "Is Bobby **first, last,** or in the **middle?**"

Jenny . . . Bobby . . . Sam

On the way to the grocery store or laundry remember to point out **new places** and **new things** to your child.

Every day keep adding to your child's new-word-list/**vocabulary.**

Tell your child the **name of everything** around you!

Check to see if he/she **remembers** the name.

Physical Activity _____

Have your child bounce a ball (with both hands)

5 times, 6 times, 7 times, 8 times, 9 times, 10 times.

Then 9 times, 8 times, 7 times, 6 times, 5 times.

5, 6, 7, 8, 9, 10

9, 8, 7, 6, 5

↓↑

Mental Activity _____

"Today is the **last** day of the week. What is its **name?**"
Make sure that your child knows
his/her whole **name.**
his/her street **address, city,** and **state.**
his/her **phone number.**
your whole **name.**
where **you work.**

BILLY THOMAS
20 CENTER STREET
WEBSTER, ALABAMA
555-6789
SUE THOMAS
STATE BANK

SUZY SCOTT
900 PARK STREET
CHICAGO, ILLINOIS
555-6543
MARSHA & BOB SCOTT
CENTER GROCERY

Put an X on the 2 boxes that are **alike.**

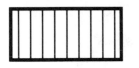

Put an X on the 1 circle that is **different**.

Physical Activity _____

Jump rope with your child today. It is a great exercise for developing skill in balance and coordination!

Parent—Did You Remember To

| HUG | READ TOGETHER | GIVE CHOICES | LISTEN | ASK QUESTIONS | PRAISE | HUG |

Day 7
WEEK
11

CONGRATULATIONS!

Name _____

Date _____

You have completed *Get Ready to Learn.*
You have been preparing your mind and body
for years of successful learning experiences.

Remember, repetition and practice are
the keys to learning.

Put this calendar on your refrigerator. Each day write in the name of the day of the week.

Sunday						

Can your child identify each shape and color?

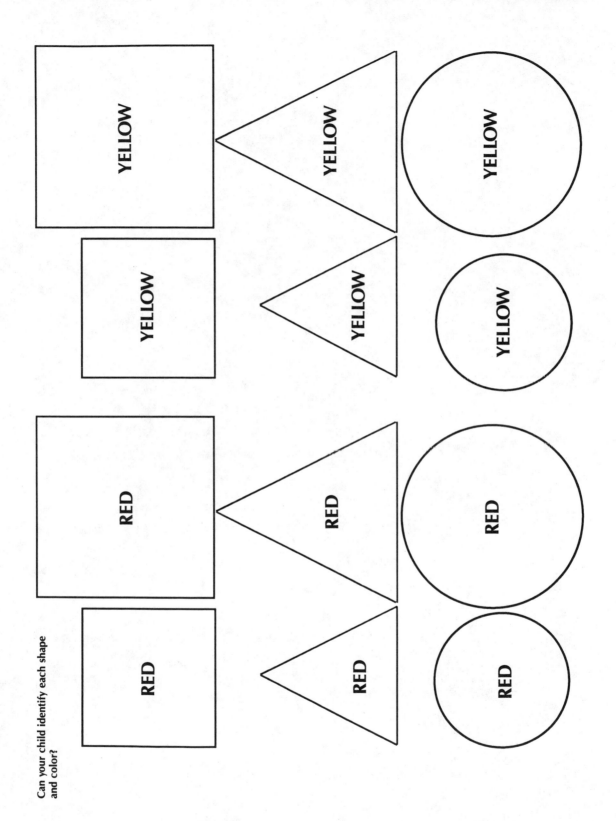

Can your child identify each shape
and color?

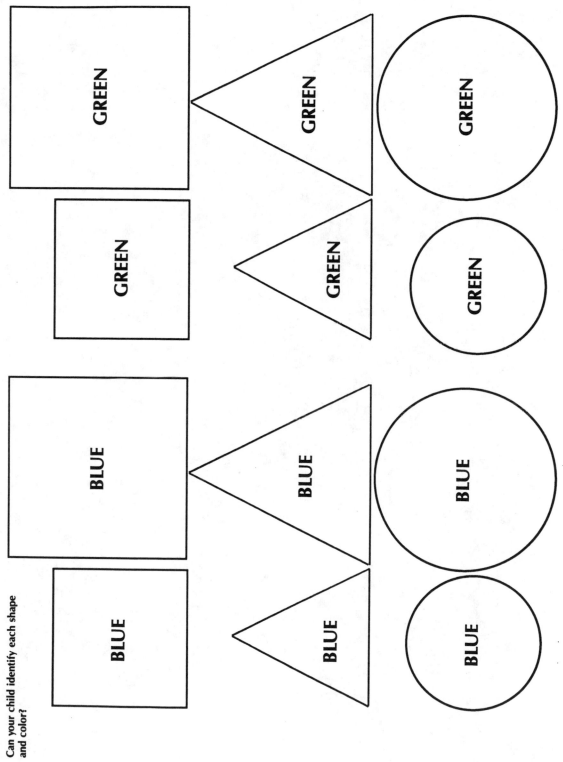

Can your child identify each shape and color?

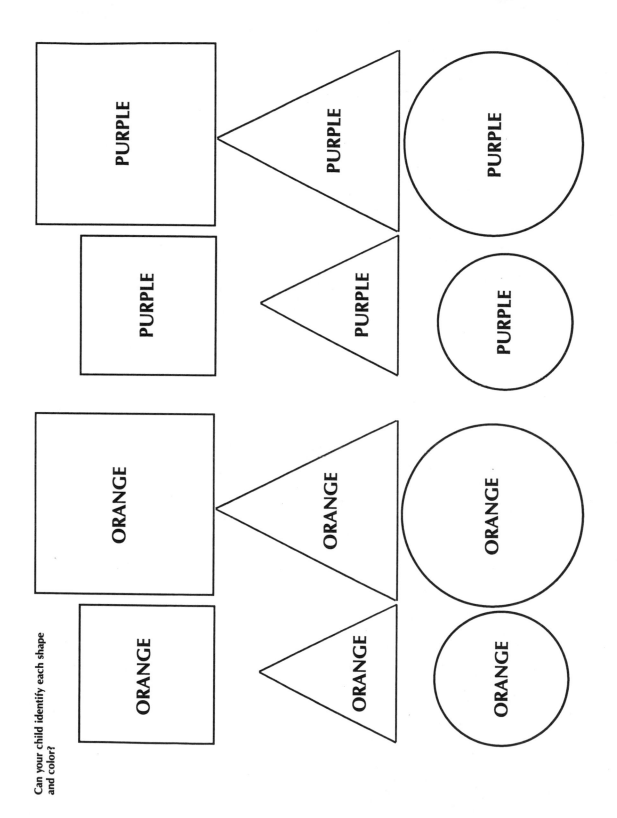

Can your child identify each shape and color?

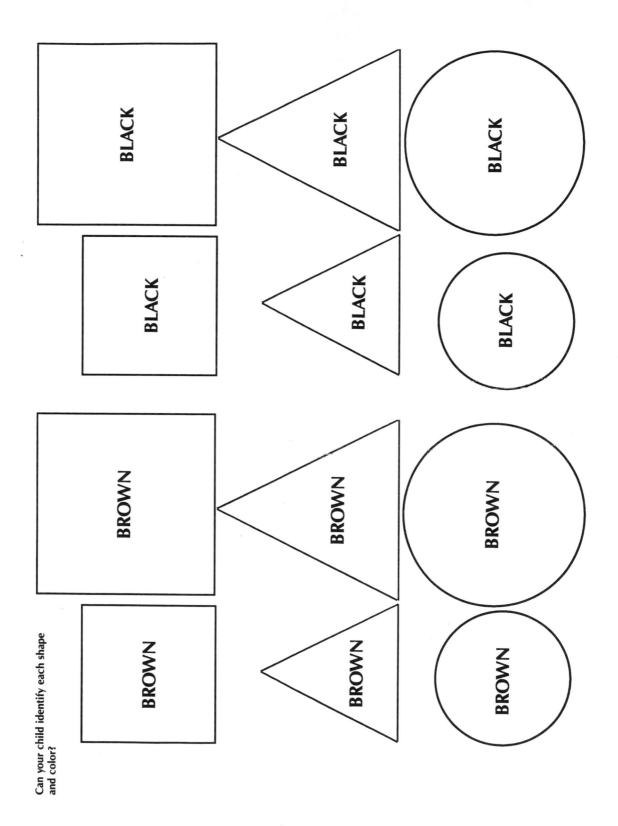

Can your child identify each shape and color?

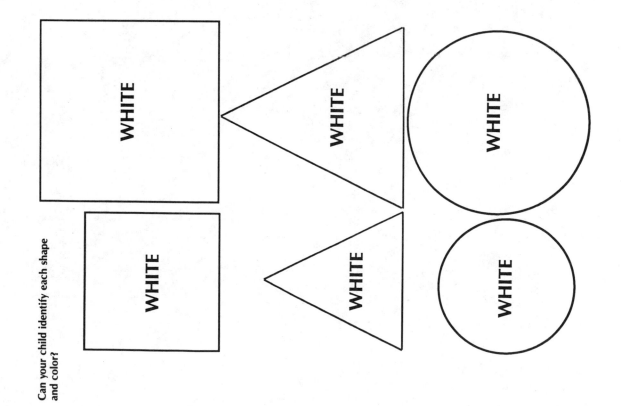

WHITE

WHITE

WHITE

WHITE

WHITE

WHITE

Nancy Champion Chupp is a certified teacher who has taught, tested, and trained children and adults for over twenty years.